Anglo-Irish Literature

Written by
Augustine Martin

"Anglo-Irish Literature"

Published by the Department of Foreign Affairs
Dublin, Ireland.

© Government of Ireland, 1980

Augustine Martin was born in Ballinamore, Co. Leitrim, in 1935, and was educated at the Cistercian College, Roscrea, and at University College Dublin, where he now holds the chair of Anglo-Irish Literature and Drama. He is Director of the Yeats International Summer School at Sligo, and has been a member of the Irish Senate since 1973. He has published widely on Yeats, Joyce, O'Casey and especially on James Stephens, to whom he has devoted a full-scale literary study. He is currently engaged on a history of the Irish short story.

Designed by Bill Murphy MSIA MSDI.
Colour separations and plates by Kulor Centre.
Printed in Ireland by The Ormond Printing Co. Ltd.

Acknowledgement

I am grateful to Dr Christopher Murray who read the
typescript and made many valuable suggestions.

Dedication

For Brefni, Gráinne, Niamh and Aengus.

Contents

Anglo-Irish Literature

1 Overleaf
Laurence Sterne (1713-1768) by Robert Ballagh.

Introduction

In order to impose a scheme on the three hundred years that fall within the scope of these fifteen thousand words I propose to divide the history of Anglo-Irish Literature into four main phases:

1. *The Colonial Phase,* stretches roughly from the Battle of the Boyne (1690) to the Act of Union (1800) and it was represented abroad by a line that ran from Congreve to Richard Brinsley Sheridan, in Ireland by a line beginning in Molyneux and Swift and ending in the last speech of Grattan in the Irish Parliament before it was dissolved.

2. *The Regional Phase,* reaches from 1800 down to the founding of the *Nation* newspaper in 1842, the period represented by the rise of the 'regional' novel with Maria Edgeworth's *Castle Rackrent* in 1800 and the emergence of the cultural nationalism of Davis, Mangan and Ferguson.

3. *The Metropolitan Phase* — when Ireland turned from colonial and regional status and became culturally a 'mother country' — covers the years from 1842 to 1922 when the Civil War ended and the new state came into being, the period that stretched from Standish James O'Grady through the Irish Literary Renaissance, the founding of the Abbey Theatre and the Easter Rising to the disillusion of the Civil War.

4. *The Contemporary Phase* takes us down to the present day.

Augustin Martin

The Colonial Phase 1690-1800

It is important from the outset to distinguish two separate but related meanings of the term 'Anglo-Irish'. Used to describe a social class and tradition it denotes the English speaking, largely Protestant, Ascendency who formed the ruling class in Ireland after the collapse of the old Gaelic order at the Battle of Kinsale and down to comparatively modern times. It is well characterised by the historian RB McDowell in his book, *Irish Public Opinion, 1750-1800,* when he writes:

Throughout the century, the Anglo-Irish preserved the spiritual and intellectual make-up of colonists, proud of their past story and of their place in the existing scheme of things, and keenly enjoying their own local life, yet all the time imitating the intellectual, political and cultural habits of the motherland.

The second meaning of the term is the literary one denoting Irish writing in the English language. The distinction is important because during this first phase the two meanings coalesce. Irish writers in English were drawn almost exclusively from the Protestant Ascendency, they saw London as their cultural metropolis and they chose their themes from that universal body of human experience that exercised the attention of their fellow Augustans in England. The playwrights, novelists, poets and satirists who migrated to London during the period were less concerned with their Irish identity than with Pope's 'proper study of mankind' or Dr Johnson's global perspectives in *The Vanity of Human Wishes:*

Let Observation with extensive View,
Survey Mankind, from China to Peru;

They were happy to belong to what Addison called 'the Republic of Letters', and their work is hardly to be distinguished in terms of language, theme or experience from that of their English counterparts.

Far from stressing their Irishness, as later writers from Thomas Moore to Brendan Behan were to do, they were sometimes at pains to conceal it. An extreme case is that of William Congreve (1670-1729) who falsified his birth date by two years — he was born in Ireland in 1672, not in Yorkshire in 1670, as is still commonly believed — in order to avoid the unfashionable implications of being 'Irish'. But though the Irish contribution to Augustan letters is of astonishing range and quality, a student of literature might be forgiven for quite overlooking the origins of its practitioners. Even the names offer little assistance — Swift, Farquhar, Congreve, Sterne, Steele, Parnell, Burke, Goldsmith, Sheridan *père et fils,* Berkeley and Hugh Kelly — the unjustly forgotton exception who forlornly proves the rule. The careers of these writers, spanning more than a hundred years, exhibit a significant pattern: early education at an Irish Protestant grammar school (education was forbidden to the native, largely Irish-speaking Catholic population), followed by a University career at Trinity College Dublin, followed by emigration to London to a place in the Church, the Temple or politics. Congreve, Berkeley and Swift went to Kilkenny College. Swift, Thomas Parnell, Berkeley, Thomas Sheridan, Goldsmith and Burke were students at Trinity. In England Steele, Swift, Burke and Richard Brinsley Sheridan entered political life; Swift, Sterne, Parnell and Berkeley chose ecclesiastical careers; Congreve, Burke and Kelly took up law. Goldsmith alone eked out an existence on Grub Street.

All of them gained easy access to social and literary circles. The Scriblerus Club founded in 1713 and Johnson's Literary Club founded in 1764 afforded them places of honour: Swift, Congreve and Parnell sat with Pope, Gay and Lord Oxford at the former while Burke, Goldsmith and Richard Brinsley Sheridan contended with Boswell, Reynolds and Charles Fox at the latter.

Indeed this expatriate tradition might be left to the mainstream of classical English literature and cut loose from its apparently tenuous Irish moorings, were it not for three oddly assorted factors that bore weightily on the scene at home and became especially salient with the dawning of the new century. These were the early and special case of Swift, the phenomenon of the 'stage Irishman' and the arrival of Thomas Moore in London at the turn of the 19th century.

The Colonial Phase 1690~1800

4

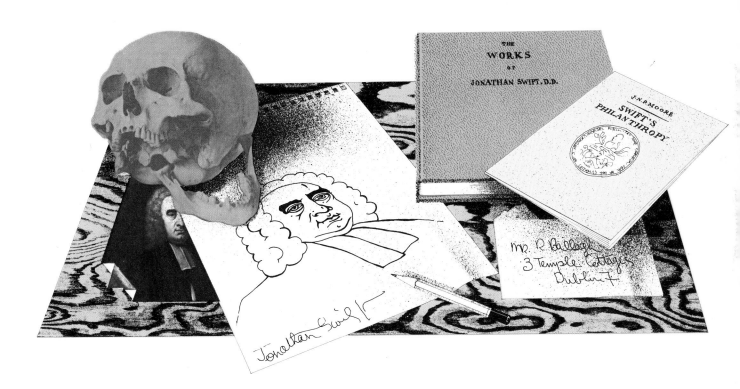

Anglo-Irish Literature

The stage Irishman had first appeared on the English scene in the figure of Captain Macmorris in Shakespeare's *King Henry V,* where a speech of his is so often taken to epitomise the 'problem of identity' of the Anglo-Irish:

Macmorris; *Of my nation! What ish my nation? Ish a villain and a bastard, and a knave, and a rascal — What is my nation? Who talks of my nation?*

The speech is probably unconcerned with any problem of identity; Macmorris is not accusing Ireland of bastardy, knavery or rascality. On the contrary his touchy national pride is hurt by the Welsh captain's superior tone so he challenges him to utter his insult: 'What are you going to call my nation — a bastard, a knave, a rascal — come on, out with it!' is probably closer to his sense. And this is the spirit in which the Irish gentleman is presented on the stage from the age of Farquhar and Congreve down to Sheridan's *Rivals,* a character compounded of national pride, irrascibility, outspokenness and generous impetuousity. Cowden Clarke wrote of Farquhar's characters in these terms:

Farquhar's gentlemen are Irish gentlemen, frank, generous, eloquent, witty, and with a cordial word of gallantry always at command.

The line is clear from Farquhar's Roebuck *(Love and a Bottle,* 1698) through Thomas Sheridan's admirable Captain O'Blunder and Hugh Kelly's Connolly in *The School for Wives* down to Richard Brinsley Sheridan's Sir Lucius O'Trigger in *The Rivals.* Side by side with the Irish gentleman type ran the Irish servant, Teague, who first appeared, resourceful and ingenious, in Sir Robert Howard's *The Committee* (1765) and survived as a popular and mostly commendable type till around 1800. He is the lineal ancestor of Boucicault's Conn in *The Shaughraun.*

In the comedy of manners which dominated the Augustan stage, the stage Irishman was a welcome variation on the humours and stock characters that made up so much of the theatre's normal traffic; however obliquely, it kept the affairs of the smaller island before a fashionable English public. And the caricature was almost universally mild and agreeable, in sharp contrast to the gross cartoons that proliferated in the later stages of the succeeding century, especially in the pages of *Punch.*

The special case of Jonathan Swift (1667-1745) arises from the fact that in 1714 — following incidentally upon a heated controversy with his countryman, Richard Steele — he returned with blighted hopes to Ireland to take up the Deanship of St Patrick's, Dublin, to die, in his own words, 'like a rat in a hole'. For reasons far too complex to discuss here, Swift, whose energies over the previous years had been funnelled furiously into British politics, began to take an increasingly vivid interest in the affairs of Dublin and Ireland. He was particularly exercised by the increasing domination of the Irish by the London Parliament, a question which had been trenchantly argued by William Molyneux (1661-1733) in a famous pamphlet of 1698, *The case of Ireland's being bound by acts of parliament in England.* This issue came to a head in the passing of the notorious Declaratory Act (the Sixth of George I) in 1720, and it is in that year that Swift's activities as a pamphleteering Irish patriot commences with his *Proposal for the Universal Use of Irish Manufacture.*

The issue of buying Irish manufactures was intimately bound up with the parliamentary issue adumbrated in the title of Molyneux's pamphlet. Repeated British enactments had curtailed Irish exports to Britain, and Irish industries, especially the woollen industry, had suffered drastically. Molyneux's contention that the British parliament had no right to legislate for Ireland without the consent of the Dublin parliament was to echo through all of Britain's colonies throughout the century having particular influence on Benjamin Franklin and other leaders of the American Revolution. Swift took Molyneux's line, calling on the Irish to support their own industries, to put an end to absentee landlordism, to resist imposed legislation and boycott imports from Britain. His slogan *'Burn everything English except their coal'* was to be repeated and adapted to many nationalistic causes in the centuries that followed.

But his prime opportunity came with the imposition of a coinage on Ireland, 'Wood's Halfpence', without the consent of the Irish Parliament. This called forth from Swift the celebrated *Drapier's Letters*, wherein he attacked the coinage and the principle of national autonomy which it violated with a ferocity and a range of rhetorical strategies seldom equalled in the history of polemical literature. The climax to the third letter is typical both in its style and implication:

Were not the people of Ireland *born as free as those of England? How have they forfeited their freedom? Is not their* Parliament *as fair a* Representative *of the* People, *as that of England? And hath not their Privy Council as great, or a greater Share in the Administration of Public Affairs? Are they not subject to the same King? Does not the same* Sun *shine over them? And have they not the same* God *for their Protector? Am I a* Free-man *in* England, *and do I become a* Slave *in six hours by crossing the Channel?*

It is important to note that by the 'people of Ireland' Swift meant the Anglo-Irish ruling class belonging to the Established Church. Not only was the vast native Catholic majority excluded from his concept of the Irish nation but the large minority of Anglo-Irish Dissenters as well. This did not prevent his words being used repeatedly in the evolving nationalist and separatist polemics of future generations.

The *Drapier Letters* so transcended their occasion as to become, like Swift's later and even greater pamphlet, *A Modest Proposal,* classics of English literature. Perhaps even more significant was the inclusion of the Wood's Halfpence affair in the Third Voyage of *Gulliver's Travels.* There the citizens of Llindalino (Dublin) defy the despotic powers of Laputa, the Flying Island, which had attempted to extort a tax from Llindalino — as from all of its other 'dominions' — without consulting the wishes of the people. The strategies of the citizens *'broke entirely*

the King's measures . . . he was forced to give the town their own conditions.' It is the first significant appearance of Irish political experience in an Irish work of fiction.

The middle years of the 18th century were marked by increasing tension between the ruling Anglo-Irish and their English counterparts, expressing itself mainly in parliamentary oratory and political pamphleteering. The popular ballad in English became especially prominent in the towns as the native Irish became gradually more articulate in the English language. As yet there is no sense of an indigenous Anglo-Irish literature but a sense of Ireland's separate destiny manifests itself in diverse ways. We find George Berkeley (1685-1753) confiding to his *Commonplace Book* that there are men *'who say that the wall is not white, the fire is not hot. We Irishmen cannot attain to these truths. The mathematicians think that there are insensible lines . . . . We Irishmen can conceive no such lines . . . I publish this . . . to know whether other men have the same ideas as Irishmen.'* Looking back from 1930, Yeats was to declare that these sentences of Berkeley's marked *'the birth of national intellect . . . the Irish Salamis.'*

Meanwhile in the English House of Commons 'Burke's great melody' thundered against the oppression of both Ireland and America. With the granting of legislative independence to Ireland in 1782, under military pressure from the Irish Volunteers, the great period of 'Grattan's Parliament' was inaugurated. Until the dissolution of that parliament by the Act of Union in 1800, Dublin underwent a grand flowering of political, literary, architectural and artistic creativity. Though the native Catholic Irish had little or no part in that activity, the last years of the century produced a number of developments that were to be of immense cultural consequence for Ireland's future These were in the first place political. The French Revolution brought in its immediate train the United Irishmen's Rebellion of 1798 in which Catholics and Protestants made common cause against British Imperialism. This was intensified five years later when Robert Emmet's rebellion added another

Anglo-Irish Literature

name to the list of romantic Irish patriots already being celebrated in a growing corpus of political balladry — Wolfe Tone, Lord Edward Fitzgerald, William Orr, Napper Tandy, Michael Dwyer, Father Murphy and Kelly of Killane.

Then there was the increasing interest in native Irish culture, the written and spoken language, the history, the music, the mythology, the literature of Irish-speaking Ireland. The Ossianic forgeries of James Macpherson in the mid 18th century had stimulated poetic and scholarly interest in the 'Celtic periphery' of Scotland, Wales and Ireland. English Romanticism tended to direct the creative impulse beyond the horizons of the Georgian city. National and regional particularity and idiosyncrasy rapidly replaced the universal perspective of Johnson and his Augustans. Gray's Bard and Burns' Cotter were quickly to be followed by the regional fiction of Maria Edgeworth and Walter Scott. And the Gothic landscapes of Walpole were to provoke an answering vision in the Irish fiction of Charles Maturin (1772-1824) and later of Joseph Sheridan Le Fanu (1814-73). Crucial to this shift in perspective were a few curious and vivid events in the last years of the 18th century.

Charlotte Brooke, in her *Reliques of Irish Poetry* (1789), published five 'Ossianic poems' with approximate, parallel translations, thus establishing the first firm bridgehead onto that mythological territory towards which Macpherson had vaguely gestured. The Royal Irish Academy, founded five years earlier, had already begun the collection and classification of Irish manuscript material which was to yield such fruit in the next century through the scholarship of O'Donovan, Petrie and O'Curry and the poetry of Ferguson and his followers. In 1792, the famous Harpers' Festival took place at Belfast, providing the inspiration for the young Edward Bunting (1773-1843) to explore Ireland and compile his great collection, *The Ancient Music of Ireland* (1796). This collection, in turn, provided both the inspiration and material for the *Irish Melodies* of Thomas Moore (1779-1852). Moore's career marks a watershed in the Irish writer's dialogue with his material and his public. True to the expatriate

tradition already well established, Moore went to Trinity and moved to London to study at the Middle Temple in 1799. But the remarkable literary career that followed differed from those of his predecessors in as far as it drew its strength mainly from Irish experience. With the recent rebellion and the Act of Union, Ireland was in the forefront of public consciousness. Moore's major theme was Ireland, her history, legends, heroes — especially Moore's friend Robert Emmet, executed in 1803 — her ruins, landscapes, memories.

Moore was strikingly typical of an age of transition. His early satires show him a late Augustan, his exotic *Lalla Rookh* an exponent of Romantic extravagance. His prose satire, *Captain Rock*, recounts the wrongs of the Irish in the idiom of dry 18th-century wit. His *Melodies* lamented and protested the sufferings of his country but brought positive delight to the fashionable, political audience at Holland House where he sang them to his own accompaniment almost nightly. He arrived in London to witness the decline of Richard Brinsley Sheridan and survived to write his official biography. But though his *Melodies* were aimed mainly at a London audience, they gradually passed into the oral tradition of his own country and proved an inspiration for poets working in the native idiom not only in their evocation of a heroic past but in their peculiarly Irish rhythms and cadences:

At the mid hour of night, when stars are weeping I fly
To the lone vale we loved, when life shone warm in
  thine eye;

That slow, wavering rhythm and delayed beat, so different from the iambic stress of traditional English poetry is to recur in the work of Callanan, Mangan, Ferguson and in the early volumes of Yeats. Thus, especially in retrospect, Moore can be seen as dominating that crossroads in Anglo-Irish literature when the 'Colonial Phase' came to an end, when the expatriate tradition took a new and distinctively Irish turn, and when Irish writers at home began to apply themselves vigorously to Irish themes while looking still to Britain for audience and readership.

*5 *Edmund Burke (1729-97), left, detail of a painting by Thomas Hickey.*

6 *Oliver Goldsmith (1728-74) by Sir Joshua Reynolds.*

7 *The poet, Tom Moore, (1779-1852) by George Mulvany.*

* *Erratum:*
Edmund Burke (1729-97) right, with Charles Fox, left, detail of a painting by Thomas Hickey

56

7

8 *Edgeworthstown House, home of Maria Edgeworth (1767-1849). The initially delapidated mansion furnished the model for Castle Rackrent.*

9 *Maria Edgeworth, aged 20, from a family portrait by Adam Buck.*

The forty years of this period are marked chiefly by the emergence of the Irish novel. In the hands of writers like Maria Edgeworth, Lady Morgan, Charles Maturin, Gerald Griffin, Thomas Crofton Croker, John and Michael Banim. Samuel Lover and Charles Lever, the Irish novel, tale and folk legend came to remarkable prominence in the British literary world. It is probably significant in terms of social history that this phase began with a writer of the Protestant Ascendancy, proceeded to novelists drawn from the Catholic middle classes like Griffin and the Banims, and eventually produced a novelist of genius, William Carleton (1794-1869), born to bilingual Catholic cottagers in Co. Tyrone and educated mostly at 'hedge schools'. The appeal of these novels to a foreign readership — apart from their intrinsic merits which varied greatly between the excellence of *Castle Rackrent* and the bathetic opportunism of *The Wild Irish Boy* — was their depiction of a world that was Celtic, outlandish, primitive, full of exotic glamour and weird idiosyncrasy. In a celebrated postscript to his *Waverley,* Scott expressed his indebtedness to Maria Edgeworth; and the entertainment of his eponymous hero at the Scottish seat of Bradwardine recalls only too vividly the drunken hospitality of Sir Patrick Rackrent. Indeed Scott's heroines, the winsome Rose Bradwardine and the majestic Flora Mac Ivor, sort well with that procession of Irish colleens that enliven the Hibernian nights of his Irish contemporaries. In turn Scott showed the Irish the way in historical fiction, though few of them came anyway near his pace. John Banim's *The Boyne Water* (1828) is perhaps the one attempt, an honourable failure, to match the energy and range of Scott's historical reconstructions.

9

There is no doubt, however, as to who dominates the first decades of the century in prose fiction. Maria Edgeworth (1768-1849) — the birthdate usually given, 1767, is almost certainly mistaken — does not seem to have realized what an innovation she had made when she entrusted the narration of her first novel, *Castle Rackrent* (1800), to the old steward of the family, Thady Quirk, for she never used that form of first person narrative again in her fiction. But *Castle Rackrent* is the first vernacular novel in the English tradition and deserves to rank with *Huckleberry Finn* as a presentation of reality from the viewpoint of a local, unlettered, 'naive' participant in the fictive world created by the novel. It is further unique in being the first sustained, imaginative critique of Irish landlordism by a writer from its own ranks. The presentation of four generations of the Rackrent family, their ignominious failure in their stewardship, the financial and moral collapse of the dynasty and the growing oppression of their defenceless and wretched tenantry was a striking achievement for a young woman of Maria Edgeworth's time and place. The rise of the narrator's son, Jason Quirk, to the agency and eventually ownership of the property is little short of prophetic in its social and historical implications. The author never quite equalled *Castle Rackrent* in vividness or originality. But her other 'Irish novels' pursue, through more conventional forms, her themes of national morale, agrarian reform, social and moral responsibility. *Ennui* (1809), her second Irish novel adopts the current convention of the romantic comedy in its plot and suffers severely from a very strong didactic purpose, a tendancy in all of Maria Edgeworth's fiction after *Castle Rackrent*. But *Ennui* has a middle section equal to her best writing for its firsthand, detailed observation of the contemporary Irish scene. Adopting a device which she may have borrowed from Lady Morgan's *The Wild Irish Girl* (1806) — and which Scott clearly appropriates in the figure of Waverley — she arranges that her hero, Lord Glenthorn, an Irish landlord educated to a fashionable life abroad, returns to his estates in Ireland and registers, by means of his journey through the country, the strangeness of the landscape and its inhabitants. The same device combines with an explicit didactic purpose in *The Absentee* (1812) where Lord Colambre's adventures take him through post-Union Dublin society and to his absentee father's estates in the midlands. There he encounters and solves the problems of mismanagement and exploitation by agents so prominent in the landscape of the 19th century. In the last of the Irish novels, *Ormond* (1817), a mildly picaresque plot carries the destinies of an attractive young Irishman to the romantic Black Island of Loch Rea with its surviving 'Gaelic' culture back to the world of the Anglo-Irish gentry on the mainland, then to the fashionable society of pre-Revolutionary France and finally home to a happy marriage and the duties of a good and enlightened Irish landlord. The theme is that of education and eventual self-knowledge.Such social concerns as Catholic and Protestant bigotry, agrarian reform and Irish identity are tributary to the young man's growth. Many commentators have rightly seen these four novels, but especially the last three, as dramatising a sense of unease about Irish identity consequent on the Act of Union, absenteeism, the rise of discontent among the Catholic majority and the passing of leadership into the hands of O'Connell and his mass agitation. As works of literature, their influence has been very powerful, stretching across France to the great Russians, and especially to Turgenev who formally acknowledged their influence.

While Scott pays generous tribute to Maria Edgeworth in his *Waverley,* he neglects to acknowledge his even greater debts to her countrywoman, Lady Morgan (Sydney Owenson), (1776-1859). Her *Wild Irish Girl* (1806) gave him the plot, *personae,*decor and theme for at least the early chapters of *Waverley.* Her novel tells of how a debauched young Anglo-Irishman is dispatched by his long-suffering father to his estates in the west of Ireland where he rapidly learns that the wild but noble peasantry give their allegiance not to him but to the Prince who still holds court in his ruined Atlantic fortress attended by his venerable antiquarian, Father John, and his supernal harp-playing daughter, Glorvina. Scott adopts the same scenario and a comparison between Chapter 22 of his novel and the Fifth Letter of Lady Morgan's will show his Scots maiden trying to outdo in costume, coiffure and harping her Irish predecessor. Glorvina's harp and costume were to become the rage of fashionable Europe. Her novel, sentimental, florid and extravagant, created a cultish interest in Ireland which was not difficult to rekindle when that 'blest pair of sirens', Cathleen ní Houlihan and Pegeen Mike O'Flaherty, came back to haunt the English consciousness with the founding of the

theatre movement a century later. Around her meagre plot, Lady Morgan, in imitation perhaps of *Castle Rackrent,* assembled a great mass of footnotes explaining and extolling the national customs to the uninitiated hero/reader, a feature of the regional novel followed also by Scott. The device was clearly acceptable to the contemporary readership and constituted one of the book's attractions, though it is laborious and embarrassing to a modern eye.

Behind the romantic extravangances of Lady Morgan's fiction lay a debate which was both real and central to her times: the question of justice and reconciliation between the two nations, the Protestant, English-speaking Ascendency culture and the Catholic, Gaelic tradition with its plaintive memories and more importunate aspirations. Her version of the Gaelic past was sentimental, more redolent of Macpherson's *Ossian* and Moore's *Melodies*—both names haunt the footnotes and text of her novel — than of any authentic scholarship. But her sense of a nation in crisis was profoundly realistic, and the best of her subsequent novels, *O'Donnell, a National Tale* (1814), *Florence Macarthy: an Irish Tale* (1818) and her historical novel, *The O'Briens and the O'Flahertys* (1827) can be read as uneasy parables in cultural patriotism. It is not surprising that Charles Maturin (1782-1824), having ignobly tried to exploit the cult she had created, with his *Wild Irish Boy* (1808), should have gone on, in *The Milesian Chief* (1812), to dramatise the conscience of a heroine, imbued also with *Ossian,* as she struggles between the demands of her English lover and the attraction of the young, barbaric Milesian in his Galway tower. The outcome of all such dilemmas, dictated as much by Romantic primitivism as by Irish patriotism, is the triumph of the Hibernian Heathcliff.

John Banim (1798-1842) and his brother Michael (1796-1874) mark the emergence of the Catholic middle class into the world of Irish fiction. Their *Tales of the O'Hara Family,* begun jointly under the pseudoyms, Abel and Barnes O'Hara, were the product of collaboration until the death of John in 1842, and were continued by Michael, though with less

10 *Lady Morgan (Sydney Owenson) in the costume of Glorvina, the Wild Irish Girl, whose harp and costume were to become the rage of fashionable Europe.*

10

11

12

11 *Michael Banim (1796-1874) by Thomas Thompson.*

12 *A scene from the 1920 silent film,* Willy Reilly and the Colleen Bawn, *which was based on Gerald Griffin's* The Collegians.

13 *A portrait of Gerald Griffin (1802-40) by Richard Rothwell.*

13

success, till his last years. While Michael stayed at home in Kilkenny to manage the family business, John followed a typical writer's career: education at Kilkenny College and at a Dublin art school followed by migration to London, where he had an initial success with his tragedy, *Damon and Pythias,* which was produced in Covent Garden by Macready and Kemble in 1821. When he and his brother began to produce their O'Hara tales, a British reading public, that had become used to Irish idiocyncrasy and romance, was now presented with the horror and violence that had for so long pervaded Irish history. *Crohoore of the Bill Hook* (1825), the first of the tales, dealt unflinchingly with the atrocities of the Catholic terrorist 'Whiteboys' of the previous century, while *The Croppy* (1826) provided a vivid and gory account of the Rebellion of 1798. The bulk of the Banims' large output was historical novels, and *The Boyne Water* (1826), written by John alone, earned for its author the title of 'The Scott of Ireland.' It hardly deserves the praise it has received by the most eminent critics even to the present day, being flawed by an improbable plot, melodramatic incident, flat characterisation and an obtrusive evangelical purpose — Orange and Green on the eve of Catholic Emancipation

Gerald Griffin (1802-40) joined his friend Banim in London and laboured long to achieve a theatrical success. Celebrity and lasting fame came to him eventually through his Irish fiction, especially his long novel, *The Collegians* (1829), which recounts in unforgettable primary colours the tragic fate of the beautiful Eily O'Connor at the hands of the swashbuckling Hardness Cregan. The melodramatic plot at its centre lent itself easily to the talents of Dion Boucicault when he adapted it for the stage as *The Colleen Bawn* (1860) and was further immortalised in Benedict's light opera, *The Lily of Killarney.*

Griffin was noted in his time for his collection of stories recorded or adapted from the oral traditions of his neighbourhood, *Holland Tide; or Munster Popular Tales* and *Tales of the Munster Festivals* (both 1827). A master of this genre was Thomas

Crofton Croker (1798-1854), whose *Fairy Legends and Traditions of the South of Ireland* (1825) was immensely successful in Britain; it was translated into German by the Brothers Grimm and is used and respected by modern folklorists. Samuel Lover's *Stories and Legends of Ireland* (1831) was a notable contribution to this increasingly popular genre which may be seen as the fore-runner of the modern Irish short story. Before moving on to the greatest practitioner of the short tale or sketch, William Carleton, one might mention the unjustly neglected Irish novels of Charles Lever, especially his finely picaresque creation, *Charles O'Malley* (1841) and Samuel Lover's full length novels, *Rory O'Moore* (1836) and *Handy Andy* (1842) which can reasonably be seen not only as inspirations to the Irish fiction of Trollope and Thackeray, but distant ancestors of the incomparable Somerville and Ross.

William Carleton (1794-1864) was in one respect exceptional to the general pattern of Irish fiction writers of this 'Regional Phase': he never went to London nor did he write with a eye to a London audience. Dublin was his metropolis and his readership was Irish. The youngest of fourteen children on his father's Tyrone farm, he was educated first locally and then at a Latin school in Dundalk with a view to the priesthood. He even set out for Munster where the best classical 'hedge schools' still flourished, but turned back because, as he alleged, he was warned against the course in a dream. His *Autobiography* published in 1896 gives a lively account of his young manhood, the influence on his life of his reading *Gil Blas* and his own picaresque adventures in his home locality and on the road to Dublin where he began his literary career in the late twenties writing for the *Christian Examiner,* a bigoted Protestant journal edited by the notorious Caesar Otway. In the first of a series of curious religious shifts, Carleton became a Protestant and his first stories, in line with the journal's evangelical policy, were virulently anti-Catholic. But no sectarian bias could disguise the power, fluency and colour with which Carleton rendered the peasant Ireland of his childhood. When these sketches and tales were revised and published as *Traits and Stories of the Irish*

14 *William Carleton (1794-1864).*

15 *Phiz, the illustrator of Dickens' novels, captures the spirt of Carleton's Ireland in his depictions of Irish life.*

16 *Malton's depictions of Dublin at the end of the 18th century contrast strikingly with the harsh realities of rural life. A number of journals sprung up and flourished there in the early 19th century.*

Anglo-Irish Literature

Peasantry (1830) and its finer Second Series in 1833 it was clear that the indigenous Irish genius for storytelling had emerged triumphantly in the English language. This was the quality applauded by Yeats a generation later, while editing a selection of Carleton's stories, describing him as the *'greatest novelist of Ireland by right of the most Celtic eyes that ever gazed from under the brow of a story-teller.'*

Despite its flaws, which include digressiveness, verbosity, polemics and melodrama, this body of short fiction gives an astonishing vision of Irish life, its rural humours, its social ceremonies, its religious divisions and the passions issuing from them, the chilling and often grotesque violence that intermittently broke out, the secret societies and the huge variety of human types and characters — priests, parsons, agents, gaugers, landlords, quacks, wiseacres, rogues and innocents. The range and energy of this portraiture sends one looking for parallels in Langland, Chaucer, or Carleton's great English contemporary, Dickens. Indeed the Dickensian blend of pathos and melodrama, of character and caricature, of social realism and social polemic — abetted in several instances by Dickens' illustrator, *Phiz* — is to be found in many of the novels, most notably *Fardorougha, the Miser* (1839), *The Black Prophet* (1847) and *Valentine McClutchy, The Irish Agent* (1847). *The Black Prophet* appears in the second year of the Great Famine and deals with the famine of 1822 which had made such a mark on the young Carleton. *Valentine McClutchy* is perhaps his most ambitious attempt to grapple with the theme of landlordism in his books. It raises the problem of the absentee landlord which had so exercised Maria Edgeworth, and the power of the evil agent or middleman, McClutchy, is the horror of Jason Quirk, murderous and rampant among a defenceless peasantry. The satire is extreme and heavy-handed with Dickensian conceptions such as Solomon McSlime, Darby O'Drive — a wicked bailiff — and a monstrous Anglican clergyman named Phineas Lucre. The saintly priest, Father Roche, may represent a certain remorse on Carleton's part for all the anti-clerical portraiture of his early fiction.

Carleton was never rich but the fact that he actually survived by his pen is evidence of the increasing literary activity of Dublin in the 1830s. Apart from the *Christian Examiner* there were *The Dublin University Magazine, The Dublin University Review, The Irish Penny Journal, The National Gazette, The Hibernian Magazine,* all of which published poems and stories and serialised new novels for an expanding readership in English. The decade, though dominated by the novel, showed the revival of interest in Irish poetry, which had been neglected in the years following Moore's *Melodies.* The Ordnance Survey, which began in the early 1830s, not only brought together the scholars, John O'Donovan (1809-61), Eugene O'Curry (1796-1862) and George Petrie (1790-1866) in a massive investigation of Irish place-names and their associated history, but it also provided employment and inspiration to the two poets who are to dominate the second half of the century and make possible the Irish Literary Renaissance under the leadership of Yeats: the Tory Protestant, Samuel Ferguson and the Catholic nationalist, James Clarence Mangan. The founding of the Unionist *Dublin University Magazine* under the editorship of Isaac Butt in 1833 marked a determination, adumbrated chiefly by Ferguson, to recover for the Protestant Ascencency the intellectual leadership of the Catholic middle classes which had so disturbingly passed to O'Connell during the successful agitation for Catholic Emancipation, achieved in 1829: *'We must fight our battle now with a handful of types and a composing-stick, pages like this our field, and the reading public our arbiter of war.'* Not less significantly, in 1831, James Hardiman published his massive *Irish Minstrelsy* in two volumes containing a large body of Irish poetry with parallel translations composed by a team of Irish scholars. In 1834, Ferguson launched, through the pages of the *Dublin University Magazine,* his ferocious attacks on Hardiman's papistry and on the inadequacy of his translations, offering, with the help of his Academy friends — O'Donovan, O'Curry and Petrie — his own superior renderings. Meanwhile Mangan was publishing in several Dublin journals his 'translations' from various languages, Irish among them. The translations of Edward Walsh and of

17 *John O'Donovan (1809-61) editor and translator of the* Annals of the Four Masters, *by Charles Grey.*

18 *George Petrie (1790-1866) antiquarian, by Mulrennin.*

19 *Eugene O'Curry (1796-1862), based on a pencil drawing by F W Burton.*

Anglo-Irish Literature

20 Jeremiah Joseph Callanan provided further testimony to a growing interest in the language while the scholarship of O'Curry and O'Donovan, was making available authentic versions of the Ossianic and Red Branch tales. These developments were given added impetus by the rise of the Young Irelanders under Davis, Mitchel, Gavan Duffy and Smith O'Brien, leading to the founding of *The Nation* newspaper in 1842. Though Ferguson never wrote for it, *The Nation* can be seen as marking a new phase in Irish writing. Unlike the *Dublin University Magazine* it was a genuinely non-sectarian platform for the expression of Irish cultural and political nationalism. It provided Davis with a platform for his best patriotic ballads, notably his resonant 'Death of Owen Roe O'Neill' and for Mangan's 'Ode to the Maguire' and 'Dark Rosaleen'. But its pivotal position is above all due to the fact that it addressed itself to an Irish readership that was nationwide and which encompassed the entire social spectrum. It thereby created a national, metropolitan consciousness, the sense of a shared culture in two languages, which was to prove the ground upon which Yeats was to base his literary movement in the last years of the century.

It is interesting to note that Gavan Duffy, having been to Australia and back, was both to aid and hinder him in the early years of that enterprise. Certainly we have no difficulty in knowing why Yeats felt obliged to declare his allegiance and name his exemplars in terms which now have become proverbial:

Know, that I would accounted be
True brother of a company
That sang, to sweeten Ireland's wrong
Ballad and story, rann and song

Nor may I less be counted one
With Davis, Mangan, Ferguson.

(To Ireland in the Coming Times, *The Rose,* 1893).

20 *Joseph Sheridan le Fanu (1814-73), master of the Gothic short story. Portrait by Robert Ballagh.*

It could be said of the Irish poet of the 19th century that he had no present, only a past and a future. Thomas D'Arcy McGee's poem 'The Celts' catches the posture of a people looking back to a golden age and forward to some new consummation. The poem begins:

Long, long ago, beyond the misty space
Of twice a thousand years
In Erin old there dwelt a mighty race,
Taller than Roman spears

and it ends by invoking Ossian, ubiquitous in the mythmaking of the times:

O, inspired giant! Shall we e'er behold,
In our own time
One fit to speak your spirit on the world,
Or seize your rhyme?

In the famine-ridden nightmare of the age, poetry tended to live between Eden and Utopia, between genesis and apocalypse. The heroic past must be retrieved to provide the inspiration for a tolerable future while blotting out the indignities of a miserable present. Mangan, Davis, De Vere, McGee, Ingram, Lawless, Todhunter, Larminie, Ferguson harped almost universally on the historical, the antiquarian, the elegiac, or gestured forward to a better world with imagery of the dawn, the spring, the Ireland of the coming times. James Clarence Mangan (1803-49) was in this, as in most things, exceptional, being remembered as much for his intensely personal, existential poems as for his elegies of Kincora or his feverish visions of Ireland's future. His adaptation of O'Hussey's Irish poem on the Maguire is justly famous, and his 'Dark Rosaleen' was to prove influential in its sponsoring of a sense of mystical nationalism that penetrated the early Yeats and was described by Lionel Johnson as *'the chivalry of a nation's faith struck on a sudden into the immortality of music.'* But his private voice is perhaps more universal, the sense of isolation and alienation from Society that finds expression in 'The Nameless One', 'Siberia' and the nightmarish 'Shapes and Signs' which have prompted some critics to compare him with Poe on the one hand and

Rimbaud's concept of the *'poète maudit'* on the other. The crisp, conversational irony of his translation from the Irish of 'Woman of Three Cows' anticipates the earthy Irish dialect in the poetry of Synge, Stephens and the later Yeats.

Samuel Ferguson (1810-86) proved even more influential. His handling of folk experience in such an early poem as 'The Fairy Thorn' was prophetic of the early Yeats in particular. But his short epics based on the Red Branch and Leinster heroic cycles opened an entire imaginative territory for his successors. The work of Yeats, Synge, Lady Gregory, 'AE', Herbert Trench and George Sigerson, in the region of heroic legend would hardly have been possible without the example of Ferguson's 'Mesgedra', 'Congal', 'Conary', 'The Abdication of Fergus MacRoy', 'The Táin Quest', 'The Burial of King Cormac' and his verse play, *Deirdre* which introduced a dramatic theme that has challenged almost every major writer of the Revival and a great many since.

His immediate disciple, however, Standish James O'Grady (1846-1928) is generally seen as the 'father of the Irish Literary Renaissance'. O'Grady's two-volume *History of Ireland* (1878-80) fleshed out the world of Cúchulain and the Ulster heroes, and his series of prose romances on the same material carried that epic vision to the market place and the class room. Indeed the material became radioactive with nationalist prophecy in the hands of Patrick Pearse and Countess Markievicz as they trained a younger generation in the rhetoric of heroic sacrifice and patriotic fervour.

As we approach the turn of the century, it is useful to look swiftly at the overall picture of Irish literary activity. The expatriate tradition of Irish drama on the London stage which we have last seen in the plays of Sheridan has continued with the comedies and melodramas of Boucicault, and more splendidly in the Wildean comedy of manners and the Shavian comedy of ideas. Dion Boucicault (1820-90) made his reputation with *London Assurance* (1841), a brilliant comedy of manners and went on to become the most celebrated playwright of his generation,

Anglo-Irish Literature

ranging from tear-jerking melodramas like *The Poor of New York* to spectaculars, strangely prophetic of the modern cinema, like *After Dark*. But perhaps the most enduring successes of his prolific career have been his Irish dramas *The Colleen Bawn, Arrah-na-Pogue* and *The Shaughraun* which appeared between 1860 and 1875.

Each of these has in the cast a resourceful Irish trickster, Myles-na-Gopaleen, Seán the Post, Conn the Shaughraun, roles played by Boucicault himself, great acting parts, in which the stage Irishman reaches his apotheosis.

The middle years of the 1890s were momentous for Irish drama. In 1894 George Bernard Shaw (1854-1950) scored a palpable hit with his satiric comedy, *Arms and the Man* in which a subversive treatment of chauvinism, snobbery and romantic love found expression in an epigrammatic dialogue of extraordinary crispness. Yeats' short poetic drama, *The Land of Heart's Desire,* shared the same bill and was ignored in the general acclaim for Shaw's masterpiece. Yeats received his countryman's success *'with admiration and hatred. It seemed to me inorganic, logical straightness and not the crooked road of life, yet I stood aghast before its energy'.* Shaw's comedy of ideas dominated the London stage — except for a period of unpopularity due to his attacks on the jingoism of Britain in the Great War — almost till his death in 1950. But in 1895 that other brilliant Dublin man, Oscar Wilde (1854-1900) produced his great comedy of manners, *The Importance of Being Earnest.* Shaw covered the first night as a critic and did not like it much, probably because it had no ideas in it, but the public then and since responded to it as one of the most perfect comedies in the tradition that had begun with Farquhar and Congreve two centuries earlier. Indeed it is hard to resist the conclusion that these Irishmen by virtue of their otherness, could catch and satirise the English in their most revealing moments and gestures. Their Irishness enabled them to pass through the barriers and obstacles of the British class system; their perceptions, formed in a different culture, were therefore alert to nuances of folly absurdity and sentimentality, which their

host society had come to take for granted as the familiar furniture of their lives. It was also in 1894 that another expatriate writer, George Moore, having spent the 1880s in Paris, brought the lessons of Zola and the French Naturalists to bear on the English novel in *Esther Waters,* a most sensitive study of an English working girl whose life is shadowed by a drunken stepfather and a husband's passion for gambling on horses. The book is still regarded by many as not only the best but the only work of naturalism in the English novel. As the Nineties drew to a close, Moore moved to Dublin where he was to become a prominent figure in the Irish Literary Renaissance.

The novel at home had declined. With the exception of Sheridan Le Fanu's Gothic tales, and William Allingham's remarkable verse fiction, *Lawrence Bloomfield in Ireland* (1864) — a witness to the persistence of the theme of landlordism in the Anglo-Irish consciousness — there is little of lasting value before the arrival of Somerville and Ross — Edith Somerville (1858-1949), and Martin Ross (Violet Martin) (1862-1915) — with their brilliant panoramic novel *The Real Charlotte* (1894) and their two dazzling books of *Experiences of an Irish RM* published in 1890 and 1908. These books, witty, perceptive, unselfcritically amused at the vagaries of the Irish temperament as seen from the saddle or from the windows of the Big House, are perhaps the last totally confident fictional testimony of the Anglo-Irish Ascendancy. They exist quite outside the Irish Literary Renaissance where Yeats and his colleagues are, at least for the moment, labouring among peasants and rebels, trying to bridge that chasm between the two nations that had been the necessary condition for the ironic vision of Somerville and Ross — as it had been for Lover, Lever and that Anglo-Irish lady who had pioneered the tradition a century before by creating Thady Quirk and letting him talk.

William Butler Yeats (1865-1939) might have chosen the expatriate path but by opting for Ireland, by adopting the politics of the old Fenian, John O'Leary, and the mythological directions of Ferguson and O'Grady, he gave the wavering

21 *A high-charged moment in a Boucicault melodrama, from an original programme.*

22 Overleaf
George Bernard Shaw (1856-1950) and

23 *Oscar Wilde (1854-1900) both by the artist Robert Ballagh.*

21

22

procession of 19th-century Irish writing the force and consequence of a literary movement. His first successful long poem, 'The Wanderings of Oisín' (1889) placed him in a line that went back to Macpherson; his prose pieces in *The Celtic Twilight* (1893) and *The Secret Rose* (1897) drew heavily on the historical and folk materials of what later came to be called the 'hidden Ireland'; and the theatre movement that he initiated with the help of Lady Gregory and others in 1899 announced itself in terms of heroic legend, rural realism, the folk imagination and the Irish language. One of his own first plays, *Cathleen ní Houlihan* (1902) proved such a sanguinary inspiration to the nationalists that he determined never to write propaganda again. His early poetry brought the fairy faith of Sligo and Galway into synthesis with Madame Blavatsky's Theosophy and McGregor Mathers' Rosicrucianism, creating a system of thought which gave Ireland the status of a holy land with a spiritual mission to the materialist world of the day.

Meanwhile, in his plays, the figure of Cuchulainn managed to combine these same spiritual values with ancient pagan energy and aristocratic contempt for the anxieties of a mercantile world. With the turn of the century, Yeats' style evolved from the vague pre-Raphaelite idiom of his early lyricism — the 'Celtic Twilight' mode as it came to be called — to a more combative, satiric language and stance where he did battle with the *'daily spite of this unmannerly town'* in controversies involving riots at the Abbey Theatre and funds to build a gallery to house Hugh Lane's paintings. This muscular irony is most in evidence in his volume *Responsibilities* (1914) where he laments that *'Romantic Ireland's dead and gone, It's with O'Leary in the grave.'* His hope for a heroic Ireland revived with the Easter Rising of 1916 which called forth a brilliant suite of elegiac poems, notably 'Easter 1916' with its celebrated refrain *'A terrible beauty is born'*. But his poetry of this period is not optimistic. The death of Major Robert Gregory, his *'dear friend's dear son',* in the Great War set him questioning the meaning of war and of heroism; the Black and Tan War, followed by the Irish Civil War, and the Russian Revolution of 1917 forced him to the conclusion that

24

25

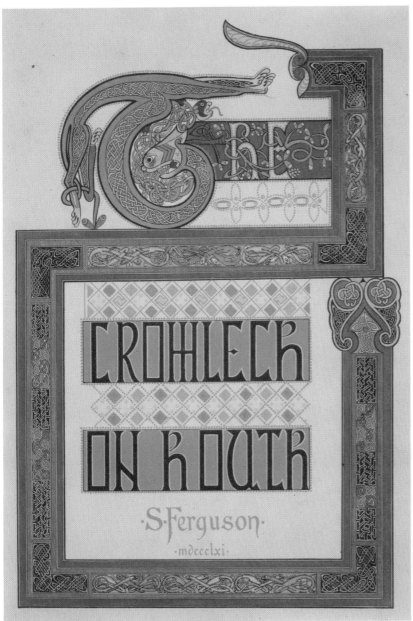

a decisive era was coming to an end in the history of the world and that the values of art, intellect and beauty, together with that aristocratic life-style which provided their guarantee and sanctuary, were at least temporarily to be swept away upon *'this filthy modern tide'*. These concerns are powerfully explored in the great lyric sequences of *The Tower* (1928) and *The Winding Stair* (1933). With his death in 1939, Yeats brought to a close a poetic career unsurpassed for range, energy and brilliance in the history of modern literature.

Yeats' Irish poetic contemporaries, though seldom approaching him in genius, were sufficiently talented and numerous, sufficiently imbued with common purposes, to constitute a genuine literary movement. George Russell ('AE') (1867-1919), though not a great writer, loomed almost as large as Yeats in the early years of the Revival. His poetry *(Homeward: Songs by the Way,* 1894), his prose *(The Mask of Apollo,* 1904) and his play, *Deirdre,* which was performed by Willie Fay's company in 1902, together with his visionary paintings of a spirit-haunted Irish landscape, did much to shape that mystical sensibility that came to be known as the Celtic Twilight. Entitled 'the poet-maker' by Oliver Gogarty, 'AE', was responsible for the launching and encouragement of a whole generation of young poets: Pádraic Colum (1881-1972) achieved early fame not only for his collection of poems *Wild Earth* (1907) but for his plays *Broken Soil* (1903), *The Land* and *Thomas Muskerry,* all performed by the new theatre company. His poetry passed swiftly into the national consciousness especially for its creation of Irish 19th-century landscape with its archetypal figures of 'The Drover', 'The Poor Scholar of the Forties' and 'The Old Woman of the Roads'. His contemporary, James Stephens, (1882-1950) burst upon the literary scene with *Insurrections* (1909), a volume of angry poems about urban squalor and social injustice interspersed with delicate nature lyrics and poems of childhood. Stephens went on to achieve a large reputation in prose fantasy with *The Crock of Gold* (1912), *The Demi-Gods* and *Irish Fairy Tales* and two outstanding collections of short stories, *Here Are Ladies* and *Etched in Moonlight.* A third protegée of

Anglo-Irish Literature

'AE' was FR Higgins (1896-1941) whose evocations of character and landscape in *Salt Air* (1924) and *A Gap of Brightness* sustained that lyric note that was so characteristic of the tradition, from its origins in Moore through the late 19th-century work of Emily Lawless, T W Rolleston, William Larminie, Joseph Campbell and Edna Carbery. Three poets are linked together by their Christian mysticism and sense of national destiny — Patrick Pearse, Thomas MacDonagh and Joseph Mary Plunkett. All three played leading parts in the Easter Rising of 1916 and died in the executions that followed.

The most visible manifestation of the Revival was the theatre movement which began in May 1899 with a double bill at the Antient Concert Rooms, under the auspices of the Irish Literary Theatre, featuring *The Countess Cathleen* by Yeats and *The Heather Field* by Edward Martyn. The two plays were in a sense prophetic of the theatre's development — Yeats' foreshadowing the poetic emphasis which the movement never quite abandoned, and Martyn's presenting the social realism which was always to be a staple ingredient in the theatre's repertoire. Between that opening night and the establishment of the Abbey Theatre on its own premises in 1904, a remarkable array of dramatic talent came forward: George Moore, Alice Milligan, Douglas Hyde — who presented the company with its first play in Irish, *Casadh an tSúgaín* in 1901 — 'AE', James Cousins, Lady Gregory, Pádraic Colum, Seamas MacManus and above all, JM Synge.

John Millington Synge (1871-1909) dominated the first decade of the Abbey's existence and is regarded by many as still its greatest dramatist. Beginning with his brilliant and disturbing one act comedy, *The Shadow of the Glen* (1903), he produced in the remaining six years of his tragically short life a series of powerful dramas of Irish rural life, culminating in the magnificent tragi-comedy, *The Playboy of the Western World* (1907) which caused riots in Dublin and ripples throughout the whole world of contemporary theatre. Synge took the speech of rural Ireland whicn had been deployed to such varied effect in fiction from Edgeworth, through Carleton to Somerville and Ross, and brought it to an intensity and eloquence unsurpassed in the language of modern theatre. Through the prism of that poetic speech he presented a vision of Irish rural life at once so desolate and hilarious, so 'passionate and simple' to use Yeats's phrase, that its Irish audiences were at once fascinated and appalled. After the patriotic fervour of Yeats's *Cathleen ní Houlihan* (1902) the wild candour of the *Playboy* was initially seen as a libel on a people weary of being caricatured in *Punch* and the British yellow press and intensely conscious of their image in the eyes of the world. But the play, and the majority of Synge's *oeuvre* passed quickly into the company's repertoire and became accepted classics of Irish theatre. Lady Gregory (1852-1932), with her remarkable energy and wide range of literary talents, made a striking contribution to the intellectual life of the times. In 1901 she co-edited the influential collection of essays, *Ideals in Ireland,* which, with its contributions by Yeats, O'Grady, Hyde,'AE', Moore and Moran, had the effect of a cultural manifesto. In 1902, she published the first of her mythological redactions, *Cúchulain of Muirtheimne,* which became a source book for Yeats and those who continued to work creatively the seam of Irish myth. On the other hand, her comedies like *Spreading the News* (1904) and *The Workhouse Ward* (1908) were unfailingly popular at the Abbey box-office.

Among the outstanding talents of the Abbey, running down to 1922, (O'Casey made his first appearance in 1923) were George Fitzmaurice, Lennox Robinson, TC Murray and Brinsley MacNamara while the popular comedies of William Boyle could always be relied on to keep the doors open as the directors awaited the arrival of a new dramatic genius. George Fitzmaurice (1878-1963) was a writer of exceptional gifts. In *The Country Dress-maker* (1907) he wrote a realistic play which transfigured the 'kitchen comedy' — rapidly becoming the commercial incubus of the new theatre — into sophisticated drama, while his delicate poetic fantasies, *The Pie-Dish* and *The Magic Glasses* exhibited a skill with dialect equal to that of Synge and a sense of the fabulous

Previous pages
24 And so the Vision Flamed and Fled, *a painting with a Celtic theme by the writer George Russell ('AE') (1867-1919).*

25 *The subject - matter and design of Samuel Ferguson's* The Cromlech on Howth *are clearly inspired by Ireland's ancient past.*

26 *Lady Gregory (1852-1932)*
by Gerald Festus Kelly.

26

Anglo-Irish Literature

comparable to that of James Stephens at his best.

Lennox Robinson (1886-1958), one of the Abbey's directors, combined civilised laughter with shrewd social commentary in such well made plays as *The Whiteheaded Boy* (1916) or *The Far-Off Hills* (1928), while in *The Big House* (1926) he explored, against the background of the fledgling Free State, the same theme of Anglo-Irish identity which had haunted the Irish literary enterprise over more than two centuries. TC Murray was the sole tragic dramatist of the period between Synge and O'Casey. This remarkable Corkman, in a creative career which stretched from *Birthright* in 1910 to *Illumination* in 1939, managed to shape out of the materials of daily rural experience a series of tragic dramas which have not yet had their critical due. *Autumn Fire* (1924), perhaps his greatest work, explores the theme handled by Eugene O'Neill in *Desire Under the Elms* with comparable strength and subtlety. Brinsley MacNamara, (1890-1963), one of the most perceptive commentators on the mores of middle-class Ireland, made his reputation not only for such sparkling Abbey comedies as *Look at the Heffernans* (1926) but for several collections of short stories and his notorious satirical novel of small-town Ireland *The Valley of the Squinting Windows* (1918). It is customary to regard the Abbey programme of these years between the death of Synge and the arrival of O'Casey in 1923 as unworthy of its great beginning, yet a glance at its record discloses a most varied and talented range of theatrical experience: poetic plays by Yeats, Fitzmaurice, Hyde, Gregory, Campbell; realistic theatre by St John Ervine, Rutherford Mayne, Murray, Shiels, Boyle, Robinson, MacNamara; importations and revivals by Sheridan, Shaw, Strindberg, Hauptman, Tagore, Goldoni, Molière; comedies of every shape and size by Stephens, Fitzmaurice, Gregory; thesis drama by Corkery, MacDonagh, Shaw — the respectable stock-in-trade of a repertory theatre going about its business, through hard times and on a lean budget. By any standards it is a defensible record.

With a few honourable exceptions such as Charles Kickham's *Knocknagow* (1879) and Emily Lawless's *Hurrish* (1886), prose fiction in the latter half of the 19th century is not remarkable for its energy or inventiveness. Its revival comes with George Moore's outstanding novel, *A Drama in Muslin* (1886), a panoramic vision of Irish life from the militancy of Land League tenant farmers through the glittering world of the Dublin 'Season' — which is presented in a manner that rivals Thackeray at his best — to a shattering climax with the Phoenix Park murders. Moore's contribution to the literary revival was however most evident in those prose master-pieces written after the turn of the century. *The Untilled Field* (1903), inspired by Turgenev's *Sportsman's Sketchbook,* marked the birth of the modern Irish short story. His novel, *The Lake* (1905), remains one of the most sensitive studies of the priestly character and vocation, while his celebrated trilogy *Ave, Salve, Vale,* (1911-1914) is an unforgettable, fictionalised history of the great years of the Irish Literary Revival.

James Joyce (1882-1941) is to Irish prose fiction what Yeats is to Irish poetry. His collection of short stories, *Dubliners* (1914), described by its author as 'a chapter in the moral history of my country', pioneered new methods of narration and new devices of myth and symbol to expose in Dublin that *hemiplegia of paralysis which many consider a city.* It remains a landmark in the history of the modern short story. His radical *bildungsroman , Portrait of the Artist as a Young Man* (1916), presented the traumata of a wilful, sensitive, Irish Catholic boy struggling through the 'nets' of family, religion, language and nationality to achieve the freedom necessary to express himself as a modern artist in words. Already in *Portrait* can be seen the unremitting experiment with language, form, symbol and technique that is to make Joyce's next novel, *Ulysses,* the most celebrated work in prose fiction of the 20th century. In it Joyce dramatises a day in the life of Dublin city. That life is registered chiefly through the sensibilities of two contrasted but mutually sympathetic *personae,* the young artist, Stephen Dedalus and the middle-aged, middle class, 'normal citizen', Leopold Bloom, Joyce's modern Odysseus, Wandering Jew, all-round contemporary man. By using what T S Elliot has

27 *A Portrait of WB Yeats (1865-1939) by Sean O'Sullivan.*

28 *John Millington Synge (1871-1909) by John Butler Yeats.*

29 *Máire O'Neill in the role of Pegeen Mike in the first production of Synge's 'Playboy of the Western World'.*

30 *James Joyce (1882-1941)*

30

described as 'the mythical method'. Joyce universalises his local experience to represent Dublin as the eternal human city. By his technique of 'the stream of consciousness', the author monitors the flux and tension of private thought and reverie passing through the minds of Dublin's citizens, and the movements of those citizens as they circle endlessly and restlessly through the veins and arteries of their city. Before he died, in 1939, Joyce having delivered to the world his 'day book' *Ulysses,* now presented them with his 'night book' *Finnegans Wake,* his imaginative 'history of the world' where experience is miraculously rendered through a language which embodies dream, nightmare, phantasmagoria, a work which has given scholars of the obscure a limitless playground for their ingenuity and erudition.

After Moore, Joyce and Stephens, the next significant contribution to the short story is Corkery's *A Munster Twilight* (1916). Daniel Corkery (1878-1964) from the start was imbued with the sentiments of the Gaelic League, devoted to Irish traditional culture, eloquently partisan on the subject of Ireland's destiny. If Moore and Joyce could be seen as rejecting the pieties of Irish life, Corkery can be seen as their champion and celebrant. It is this sense of acceptance which gives such force and fervour to the best of the stories in *A Munster Twilight* and even more particularly to his pulsating sketches of the Black and Tan War in *The Hounds of Banba* (1920). These very virtues betray him frequently to sentimentality and special pleading in his weaker or more self-indulgent fictions. When he moves beyond the special allegiances of Irish politics or culture he can write with extraordinary power of the realities of country life, as he does in his finest collection, *The Stormy Hills* (1929). His two critical works, one on Gaelic Ireland in the 18th century, *The Hidden Ireland* (1925), and the other on *Synge and Anglo-Irish Literature* (1931) continue to raise fruitful controversy, wherever the subject of Irish literary culture and national identity come up for serious discussion.

Seumas O'Kelly (1881-1918) began his writing career with an Abbey success, *The Shuiler's Child*

in 1909, but went on to even better work in fiction, especially in the short story, with his masterpiece, *The Weaver's Grave* (1919), wherein the search of a young widow for the exact location of her deceased husband's proper burial place engages the energies of a whole parish, raising every imaginable question of life and death, youth and age, tradition and change, decay and fertility, time and eternity.

As a political backdrop to these works, one may note the great lock-out of 1913 when Larkin and Connolly pitted the workers of Dublin against the employers led by William Martin Murphy; the Lane Pictures controversy wherein Yeats and his colleagues battled with the Dublin Corporation for its slowness in providing a gallery for Lane's collection of Impressionist paintings; the Rising of 1916 which inspired Yeats to some of his most memorable poems, notably 'Easter 1916' and which provoked James Stephens to write his superb memoir of the street fighting, *Insurrection in Dublin;* the Black and Tan War which raged between 1919 and 1922 when the Truce and Treaty were agreed and the Free State came into being. The Civil War that ensued is more usefully seen as the beginning of a new rather than as the end of an old chapter in the evolution of the Irish literary consciousness.

The Contemporary Phase

It is a commonplace of literary criticism that before the Civil War, Irish writing tended to be romantic and after it, ironical. The change is wryly caught in Benedict Kiely's comment that the 'terrible beauty' of a poets' rebellion had given birth merely to 'a grocers' republic'. The new state failed signally to answer to the Utopian projections of the poets. What had been foreseen in metaphors of the dawn, the Spring, the rose tree blossoming, the young girl with the walk of a queen, did not materialise in the severe, pious and frumpish figure of the new Ireland. For a start the chivalrous conduct of the Easter Rising, inspired by the stirring plea of the Proclamation that no one dishonour its cause by 'cowardice, inhumanity or rapine' was soon qualified by the ugliness of the Civil War. The shadow of that internecine conflict affected most writers of the new generation, and it returns in curious ways in the decades that followed — most notably in a poem like *Nightwalker* (1968) whose author Thomas Kinsella, was not born for six years after the event.

One poetic career that might aptly illustrate the change in sensibility is that of Austin Clarke (1896-1974) who began his career in 1916 with an Ossianic poem. Pupil of Douglas Hyde and successor to the executed Thomas MacDonagh as lecturer in English at University College Dublin, Clarke went on to write poetic plays, historical novels and a body of lyric poetry exploring what he himself termed 'the drama of racial conscience'. Like Yeats, and unlike his contemporary Patrick Kavanagh, Clarke had a historical consciousness. The world which he inhabited and expressed was for him a product of atavistic forces, historical legacies and religious imperatives which produced a special type of human sensibility. As with Stephen Dedalus, the artist in Clarke resented the domination of the Roman Catholic Church and the thought patterns of British culture. Political freedom from Britain had brought for the artist no freedom of intellect. Instead it had brought the notorious Censorship Board of 1928 against which Clarke directed his satiric fire-power:

Burn Ovid with the rest. Lovers will find
A hedge-school for themselves, and learn by heart

All that the clergy banish from the mind
When hands are joined and heads bow in the dark.

But Clarke cultivated 'the Irish mode' in poetry, working with cunning and intensity the prosodic patterns of Gaelic verse into his own elaborate poetry, exploiting the retrospect of the Celtic Romanesque to explore and frequently to indict an unsatisfactory present. Clarke's technical innovations have been visibly influential in the work of his successors to the present day.

Patrick Kavanagh (1904-67) on the other hand, rebelled against the tyranny of 'Irish tradition', attacked as 'phoney' the concept of an Irish Literary Revival and refused his allegiance to a Gaelic past:

Culture is always something that was,
Something pedants can measure
Skull of bard, thigh of chief,
Depth of dried-up river.

Kavanagh's most ambitious work was *The Great Hunger* (1942), a long poem expressing the cultural, material and sexual deprivation of a bachelor living on a small farm in rural Ireland, a work remarkable for its tragic insight and compassion; its comic counterpart is his novel, *Tarry Flynn* (1948). Equally memorable are Kavanagh's 'canal bank' poems published in the Fifties expressing a new sense of Christian acceptance and peace with nature and the world. The generation of Clarke and Kavanagh was not outstanding for its poets. On the home scene Donagh MacDonagh, Patrick MacDonagh, Padraic Fallon and Robert Farren continued to develop a poetry which relied chiefly on Irish sources and models for its inspiration. The expatriate tradition developed along two paths. The Northern Irish poets, Louis MacNeice and WR Rodgers, operated out of London with frequent sortees into their Irish background for theme and image, while John Hewitt (b.1907) wrote consistently as an Ulsterman of 'planter stock' despite his exile in the English midlands — until his return, on retirement to the midst of a troubled Belfast. The second 'expatriate' group are defined by Samuel Beckett in his remark that contemporary

Anglo-Irish Literature

Irish writers could be divided into 'the antiquarians and the others'. The latter include Beckett himself — now far more famous for his prose and drama — and Thomas McGreevy, Brian Coffey and Denis Devlin, all of whom travelled widely, absorbed and excogitated a larger, and at times selfconscious, European sensibility. Denis Devlin (1908-59) in particular has built an enduring reputation for his authoritative translations of Saint John-Perse and for such fine original poems as 'Lough Derg' and 'The Heavenly Foreigner'. In the same tradition might be included Devlin's distinguished younger contemporary, Valentin Iremonger.

What might be seen as the new movement in Irish poetry began in the Fifties with the founding of the Dolmen Press and the arrival of Thomas Kinsella (b.1928) whose reputation continues to grow as his formidable output increases. If only for his wide imaginative reach he dominates the poetic scene. Some of his most anthologised poems like 'Mirror in February' or 'The Secret Garden' declare themselves in universal terms, while a poem such as *Nightwalker* (1968) is minutely and intensely wedded to its Irish context. His great rendering in prose of the *Táin,* Ireland's major epic, is witness not only to his concern with a cultural heritage, but to the striking intellectual seriousness and rigour with which he goes about the creative task.

Prominent among Kinsella's immediate contemporaries are two outstanding poets, Richard Murphy (b.1927) and John Montague (b.1929). Both writers exhibit a global perspective linked to an obsessive concern for the particularity of Irish history and landscape. Montague's elaborate sense of tribal' identity is best dramatised in his remarkable lyric suite, *The Rough Field* (1972) while, Murphy, in a work of equal scope and similar intention, *The Battle of Aughrim* (1968), explores his Anglo-Irish ancestry and its contemporary implications in terms of that crucial event of Irish history. Pearse Hutchinson (b.1927), because of his slender output in original poetry, translations from Irish and versions of the Catalan, has not done full justice to his remarkable lyric gift, while Anthony Cronin (b.1925) as a fulltime man of letters has

spread himself over, poetry, fiction, memoirs, criticism and literary journalism. In an ambitious poem, *The Weekend of Dermot and Grace* (1964), the bilingual writer Eugene Watters (b.1925) has combined the mythic pursuit of Diarmuid and Gráinne with an eloquent contemporary response to the bombing of Hiroshima. Seán Lucy (b.1931), with his strong Munster sense of locality and tradition, is equally known for his epigrammatic commentary on the social scene as for his sensitive translations from the Irish. Basil Payne (b.1928) is the natural successor of James Stephens for his hard-edged cameos of Dublin and its human idiocyncrasies. Brendan Kennelly (b.1936) also wrote vividly of Dublin life and character in such early poems as 'The Fool's Rod' and 'Johnny Gobless', but an even greater strength is exhibited in the title poem of his distinguished 1964 volume, *My Dark Fathers,* where the ancestral night of history looms as a background to the play of an extremely modern poetic sensibility.

Of the poets who came to prominence in the Sixties, the Derry poet, Seamus Heaney (b.1939), was the most immediately arresting and has since proven the most consistently powerful. His first volume, *Death of a Naturalist* (1966), found its way into those regions of reality and imagination which his poetry has since made legendary, the Ulster bogs with their immense symbolic suggestiveness, the echoing wells, the proliferating flaxdam and all the gear, tackle and trim of immemorial farmlife. So compellingly were these emblematic realities established in the early volumes that they could be fused with the bog rituals of Denmark to provide a resonant symbolism for war, politics and tribal atavism when the Northern 'Troubles' broke in 1969. In creating his own poetic cosmos through a language and imagery that answers uniquely to his life and needs, Heaney has placed himself in the front rank of poets writing in English today.

In a manner not dissimilar from that of Kinsella in the Dublin of the Fifties, Heaney has found himself at the head of a school of Ulster poets which includes Michael Longley, Derek Mahon, Séamus Deane, James Simmons and younger poets like Frank Ormsby and Paul Muldoon. The word 'school' is

31 *Austin Clarke (1890-1974).*

32 *The view from Patrick Kavanagh's canal bank seat.*

'Leafy-with-Love Banks and the green waters of the canal, Pouring redemption for me . . .'

31

32

risky even in a condensed survey such as the present booklet undertakes, and the apparent sympathy between the aims of these writers may be largely due to the violent experience out of which they write. This world has evoked from James Simmons (b.1933) such superb ballads as 'Claudy' and 'A Ballad of Jerry Kelly' and from Frank Ormsby (b. 1947) a poem as deft and grievous as 'Spot the Ball'. From Séamus Deane (b.1940) it has extorted a most subtle and passionate volume of poems, *Gradual Wars* (1972), a work in which the nerves of language are stretched between private feeling and communal anguish. While Michael Longley (b.1939) in 'A Letter to Three Irish Poets' explores the 'lethal thoroughfare' of his quotidian Belfast, and all its desolating implications for the concept of a shared Irishness. The work of Derek Mahon (b.1941) dramatises the tug between the local and universal; *Night-Crossing* (1968), *Lives* (1972) and *Snow Party* (1975) exhibit a strikingly modern sensibility through a most formidable poetic technique.

Among the southern Irish poets to register the tension and unease of the times is Eavan Boland (b.1945) who has distilled in her volume, *The War Horse* (1975), a coherent and eloquent myth for the primal apprehensions that underlie the most insulated lives. Her achievement is typical of a decade which has seen a flowering of poetic talent: the bilingual poets Michael Hartnett and Conleth Ellis; Eiléan ní Chuilleanáin, Trevor Joyce, Augustus Young, Donal Murphy, Richard Ryan, Michael Smith, Brian Lynch, Paul Durcan, Desmond Egan, Sidney Bernard Smith, Hugh Maxton, Paul Murray, John F Deane and the strikingly gifted Aidan Carl Mathews (b.1956) who began to win poetry awards while still an undergraduate at University College Dublin.

Sean O'Casey's *The Shadow of a Gunman* (1923) announced not only a dramatist of original genius but a sensibility well attuned to the temper of the times. Donal Davoren, the pathetic anti-hero of the title rang down the national curtain on the heroic fantasies of the previous decade. His mood was to dominate the Irish theatre in the years that followed, in the ironies of Denis Johnston, Paul Vincent

Carroll, the latter plays of O'Casey himself and the mocking vision of Brendan Behan in his *Hostage.* O'Casey was the fulfillment of an Abbey dream, a working class writer from the Dublin tenements delivered almost full-grown to a theatre workshop which from its earliest days had fostered the ideal of art as co-operation. While inheriting some of Synge's irony, O'Casey was also heir to his poetry and could fashion from the dialect of the Dublin streets a new theatrical language that could move rapidly between laughter and pathos to produce a new concept of tragi-comedy. The *Shadow* was followed by his remarkable drama of the Civil War, *Juno and the Paycock* (1924) and to complete his 'Dublin Trilogy', by *The Plough and the Stars* (1926) in which the Rising of 1916 is refracted through the lives of a tenement community who must endure the casual horrors of urban warfare for its duration. As a document on modern warfare these plays are of enduring interest. For the dazzling range of acting parts they provide, from the lyrical clowns like Joxer, Captain Boyle, Seamus Shields, Tommy Owens, Fluther Good and the comic socialist, the Covey, to the biblical eloquence of Bessie Burgess and the tragic strength of Juno Boyle they make irresistible theatre. O'Casey's unfortunate break with the Abbey resulting from Yeats' rejection of his controversial war play, *The Silver Tassie,* in 1928 is now a commonplace of theatre history. The experimental drama of his subsequent years still awaits an adequate theatre, though Abbey productions of *Purple Dust, Cocka-Doodle Dandy* and *The Star Turns Red* in recent years have disclosed unexpected histrionic power in the dramatist's middle and later work where an increasingly radical vision of society finds expression through a daringly innovative dramaturgy.

It seemed that the Abbey had set its face against experimental theatre because in the same year, 1928, it rejected Denis Johnston's expressionist drama *The Old Lady Says 'No'* because the director, Lennox Robinson, 'couldn't handle all the choruses and the comings and goings.' It was a challenging play with a deluded actor in the role and costume of Robert Emmet moving through the unheroic Ireland of the new Free State. The Abbey, in an inspired

The Contemporary Phase

Among the many notable contemporary Irish poets are:

33 *Richard Murphy (b. 1927)*

34 *John Montague (b. 1929)*

35 *Thomas Kinsella (b. 1928)*

36 *Seamus Heaney (b. 1939)*

33
34

35
36

Anglo-Irish Literature

gesture, handed on the script to the newly formed Gate Theatre with a small subsidy. There it received a brilliant modernist production from Hilton Edwards with Michael MacLiammoir in the lead and became, over the decades, part of the Gate's classic repertoire. Had the Abbey admitted its limitations and dealt similarly with O'Casey the course of Irish theatre history might have been transformed.

Though the Abbey's policy was conservative, based in fact on Yeats' preference for 'good bad plays rather than bad good plays', it continued to attract talented playwrights. Denis Johnston's *Moon in the Yellow River* dealt subtly with the conflicting forces of tradition and technology arising out the new hydro-electric power scheme, and subsequently his *Dreaming Dust, The Golden Cuckoo, Strange Occurence on Ireland's Eye* and *The Scythe and the Sunset* appeared to enliven the repertoire of different Dublin theatre companies. Teresa Deevey (1903-63) made her Abbey debut with *The Reapers* (1930) and a recent revival of her *Katie Roche* (1936) confirmed her skill with dialogue and her subtle sense of female characterisation.

The most striking new talent of the Thirties was Paul Vincent Carroll (b.1900), whose best play, *Shadow and Substance* went on at the Abbey in 1937, and became one of the few Irish plays to conquer Broadway. *The White Steed* (1938) came close to its predecessor in intellectual seriousness and dramatic power, but Carroll's later work tended towards sentimental comedy and whimsy. MJ Molloy (b.1912) also began vividly and promised well with *Old Road* (1934) and *The King of Friday's Men* (1948), in both of which he produced a muted poetry from the rural Galway speech of his characters. Molloy's career was interrupted by the Abbey fire of 1951 when the theatre had to go into exile at the Queen's music hall. There, in 1953, Molloy's social drama, *The Wood of the Whispering* and his moving one-acter of the Famine, *The Paddy Pedlar,* had their first productions. Walter Macken (1916-67) also began at the old Abbey with *Mungo's Mansion* (1946) and put on his later plays, *Home is the Hero* (1952) and *Twilight of a Warrior* (1955) at the Queen's, before turning his considerable talent

to fiction where it is far less powerfully deployed.

Before the fire the Abbey had done little to cultivate poetic drama. Only one original drama by Yeats appeared on its boards in the Twenties, a dance play, *Fighting the Waves* (1929), done in collaboration with Ninette de Valois, though in the Thirties his prose play on Swift, *The Words Upon the Window Pane* (1930) and his Noh Play, *The Dreaming of the Bones* (1931) with its overtly nationalistic theme, had modest successes. *The Resurrection* (1934) and *Purgatory* (1938) tended to perplex those Dublin theatre-goers who attended, though *Purgatory* prefigures *Godot* and the existentialist theatre of Samuel Beckett. The Abbey was not especially concerned with poetic drama despite its production of Roibéard Ó Faracháin's *Assembly at Druim Ceat* and *Lost Light* in 1943 and Austin Clarke's *Black Fast* in 1941. To deal with this need, in 1938, Austin Clarke, Ó Faracháin, Ria Mooney and Cyril Cusack founded the Dublin Lyric Theatre and the Dublin Verse-Speaking Society which concentrated on productions of verse drama through the following years in the Peacock Theatre and on Sunday nights at the Abbey and even more significantly on Radio Éireann where the Radio Éireann Players developed a distinctive style in poetic drama. This concerted movement gave scope to Austin Clarke's *Son of Learning* (1945), *The Flame* (1941), *The Kiss* (1942), to Donagh MacDonagh's *Happy as Larry* (1941) which went on to triumph at the Mercury and later at the Criterion, London, in 1947. The Gate produced Clarke's *Sister Eucharia* in 1939. The Lyric Theatre Belfast was founded by Mary O'Malley with the specific mission of producing poetic drama and has, to the present day, given both inspiration and support to those who wish to provide a sanctuary for this essential part of the Irish theatrical heritage. With the opening of the Abbey in its new building in 1966 and its finely equipped experimental Peacock Theatre in 1967, the theatre has made it a practice to put on imaginative revivals of Yeats' drama as well as occasional productions of poetic plays by writers like Louis MacNeice and George Fitzmaurice.

The great successes of the Fifties were Samuel

Some of the great names of the 20th-century Irish theatre

37 *Seán O'Casey (1880-1964)*

38 *Samuel Beckett (b. 1906).*

39 *Brendan Behan (1923-64), by Robert Ballagh.*

40 *Hugh Leonard (b. 1928).*

37
38

39
40

Anglo-Irish Literature

Beckett, Brendan Behan and John B Keane, three sharply contrasted talents whose theatrical origins were all outside the official Irish theatre. Beckett's late vocation for drama — his first creative work was a collection of short stories, *More Pricks than Kicks* (1934) — appeared with the French version of *Waiting for Godot* in Paris, 1953, which had its English-language *première* in Dublin's tiny Pike theatre in 1955. But though Beckett's drama, especially his language, has its roots in Dublin experience, his bleak vision of man's cosmic absurdity transcends any limiting sense of local or national culture. It was also at the Pike Theatre that Brendan Behan (1923-64) made his theatrical debut with his celebrated prison drama, *The Quare Fellow* (1954) which had, in earlier drafts, been rejected both by the Gate and the Abbey. The play's intrinsic merits of shrewd characterisation and racy dialogue were greatly enhanced by its timing. It transferred to London just as the agitation against capital punishment was at its height, so that Behan's theme caught the public mood and achieved instant commercial and critical success. His later play, *The Hostage,* adapted in collaboration with Joan Littlewood from its conventional Irish language original, *An Giall,* scored an even greater hit in London and New York. Apart from his powerful memoir, *Borstal Boy* (1958), Behan did little else to fulfil his great potential before his early death in 1964.

John B Keane (b.1928) conquered the parish halls of Ireland in 1959 when his folk melodrama, *Sive,* took all the awards at the National Amateur Drama Festival and rapidly became one of the most performed plays of its generation. In the works that followed Keane developed a vision, both sharp and compassionate, of Irish country life and character, especially of the tendancy to deflect the sexual energies into power, greed, sanctimony, cruelty and land hunger. The character of Bull McCabe in Keane's finest play, *The Field* (1965), matches anything in Irish theatre from Synge's Maurya to Brien Friel's Cass Maguire.

Hugh Leonard (b.1928) began his career in the Fifties with unremarkable Abbey plays like *The Big Birthday* and *A Leap in the Dark*. His uncanny sense of theatre linked, as it is, with his eye for social nuance has made him one of Dublin's most successful playwrights of recent times. His deft adaptations of Joyce and others, notably his celebrated *Stephen D,* have tended to overshadow such fine original plays as *Madigan's Lock, Walk on the Waters* and *The Poker Session,* but the spectacular Broadway success of *Da* in 1978 put his merit as an original dramatist quite beyond question.

Brian Friel (b.1929) achieved world recognition with his superb fourth play, *Philadelphia, Here I Come* (1964) a most moving comi-tragic study in which the power of memory over fact, the tension between the inner and the outer personality, the sense of regret for lost innocence coupled with the thirst for experience, are all subsumed into the theme of exile. Among Friel's later successes have been *The Loves of Cass Maguire* (1966) — which explores these same obsessive themes from an opposite perspective — *Lovers* (1967) and his complex, challenging *Aristocrats* which had its Abbey *première* in 1979.

The drive for innovation and formal experiment so evident in Friel has been characteristic of the modern Abbey. Thomas Murphy (b.1936) began his career with a most arresting study of Irish exiles in Coventry, *Whistle in the Dark* (1961), which had an enormous success on London's West End. Since his return to Ireland he has utilised the technical resources of the Abbey for such symbolic dramas as *The Morning after Optimism* (1971), and *The Sanctuary Lamp* (1976). Thomas Kilroy (b.1934) established his reputation with *The Death and Resurrection of Mr Roche* (1968) a study of human frustration in Dublin's flat-land and went on to *Talbot's Box* (1978) which explores the enigma of sanctity in a surreal drama that drew critical applause on its London production at the Royal Court. Tom MacIntyre, on the other hand, has achieved notable effects with dance, mime and ballet in such plays as *Jack Be Nimble* (1976) and his daring treatment of the Salome theme in *Find The Lady* (1977). Still more recently the arrival of

41 *Liam O'Flaherty (b. 1897-).*

42 *Flann O'Brien (1912-66).*

43 *Francis Stuart (1902-).*

44 *James Plunkett (b. 1920).*

41
42

43
44

a,b,c

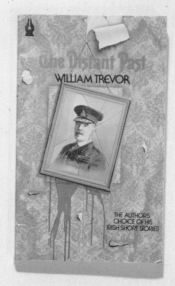

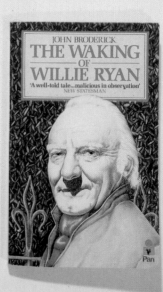

d,e,f

45
g,h,i

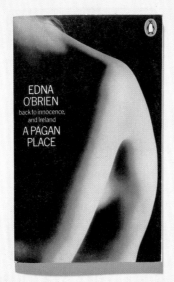

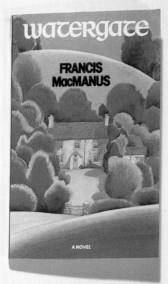

j,k,l

Anglo-Irish Literature

three outstanding young playwrights augurs well for the theatre's continued relevance and vitality. These are Stewart Parker *(Catchpenny Twist, Spokesay)*, T. Graham Reid *(The Death of Humpty Dumpty)* and Bernard Farrell *(I Do Not Like Thee, Dr. Fell)*

O'Casey and Behan have found interesting successors in such writers as Sé Sheridan whose drama of the Dublin unemployed, *Mobile Homes,* (1976) at the Project and his brother, Peter Sheridan whose *No Entry* (1976) and *The Liberty Suit* (1977) appeared when Heno Magee's *Hatchet* was exploring the tensions of Dublin's gang warfare on the boards of the Abbey.

Among the Gate's more assured dramatists have been Father Desmond Forrestal who exhibited a fine sense of history in his *Titus Oates and the Horrid Popish Plot* (1972) and Joe O'Donnell whose mood piece, *The Lads* (1971), was a further investigation of the world revealed in Kilroy's *Death and Resurrection of Mr Roche.*

The most spectacular development in fiction in the post-revolutionary period was in the short story with the emergence of Liam O'Flaherty, Elizabeth Bowen, Frank O'Connor, Seán O'Faoláin and, somewhat later, the great modern master of the form, Mary Lavin. In a period of social unrest, uncertainty and disillusion, the short story, with its emphasis on personal vision, fragmentary experience, the isolated lyrical or dramatic moment, was uniquely responsive to the needs of the time. The novel, stunned perhaps by Joyce's monumental affront to the form in *Ulysses* (1922), went temporarily to ground, or took refuge in fantasy and social satire as in Eimar O'Duffy's *King Goshawk and the Birds* (1926). Liam O'Flaherty (b 1897) was to some extent exceptional. Though his reputation will probably rest more emphatically on his short stories, his achievements in the longer form at this period will certainly endure: his archetypal evocations of Aran in *The Black Soul* (1924) and *Skerrit* (1932), his excellent historical novel, *Famine* (1937) and his memorable characterisation of Gyppo Nolan in *The Informer* (1925), which appeared as O'Casey was putting out his own dramatic version of a Dublin

traumatised by war. Some of his short stories, 'The Sniper' and 'The Mountain Tavern' deal with the same violent theme, but his genius in the shorter form is most manifest in his evocations of island life, the ritual of the seasons, the movements of animals and of men going about their primeval tasks in unison with nature. Here he evolves a sort of story subtly calculated to catch the rhythms of the universe at definitive moments of stress, climax and intensity, in language that is spare, supple and miraculously adjusted to its themes and moods.

Elizabeth Bowen (1900-73) left Ireland early and entered on a literary career which swept free of the local, social or political obsessions of the new State. Her achievement in the novel is grounded in a more cosmopolitan sense of identity and experience. Ireland looms large, however, in her affectionate and elegiac account of her Cork mansion, *Bowen's Court* (1942), and the generations who lived there before its dissolution. In her recently published *Collected Irish Stories* (1979) a remembered Irish landscape provides the material for a vivid suite of tales.

The Thirties are dominated by Frank O'Connor and Seán O'Faoláin, both rebellious disciples of Corkery who receives affectionate but not uncritical homage in each of their autobiographies. Frank O'Connor (1903-66) began his career in the short story with *Guests of the Nation* (1931) a volume which took its theme and mood from the title story, an intense and compassionate account of how two young Irish guerillas are forced to execute British prisoners in reprisals. The sense of compunction, almost of self-disgust, in the mind of the narrator emphasises how far the creative sensibility had come from Corkery's feverish enthusiasm for battle in *The Hounds of Banba* a decade before. The note is disturbingly similar to that of O'Flaherty in the last crescendo of 'The Mountain Tavern' and the disillusion of O'Faoláin's hero in the title story of *Midsummer Night's Madness* where the revolution grown sour has already bred, in the character of Stevie, the hypocritical and retributive moralism of the new middle classes. O'Connor's work over the succeeding decades ranged energetically over

45 Previous pages
Best-selling works by some of Ireland's internationally known contemporary authors.

fiction, biography, translation from the Irish, theatre and literary criticism. His stories of childhood have made him a world reputation with every sort of reader. But one suspects that his most enduring achievement is in a small body of superlative short stories distilled out of common experience, 'The Lucys', 'The Bridal Night', 'The Majesty of the Law', 'Uprooted', 'In the Train', 'The Long Road to Ummera' and 'The Wreath.' These alone place him among the great masters of the form.

Seán O'Faoláin (b.1900) followed his first volume with the first of his three novels, *A Nest of Simple Folk* (1933), which took in three generations of Irish life and had as its culmination the Rebellion of 1916. Of all Irish writers he has shown most persistence in trying to penetrate the national character, especially in its ambiguous commitment to Catholicism. This preoccupation has resulted in such intense studies of religious disaffection as that of Corney Crone in the second novel, *Bird Alone* or such an exquisitely lethal short story as 'The Man Who Invented Sin.' His determination to wrench Irish society into the mainstream of European thought led to his brilliant and fighting editorship of *The Bell* through the Forties, and has frequently tempted him towards oblique homiletic in his stories — not always to their detriment. One of O'Faoláin's chief collaborators on *The Bell* was the socialist writer Peadar O'Donnell (b.1893) among whose novels *Islanders* (1928), a vivid drama of island life off Donegal, is perhaps the most memorable.

Mary Lavin (b.1912) on the other hand has scarcely deviated from fiction since her first volume, *Tales from Bective Bridge* (1942), and though she has written finely in the longer form, notably *The Becker Wives* (1946), she has made the short story almost exclusively her vehicle. The *Collected Stories,* now running to three volumes, disclose a genius of extraordinary psychological richness and technical resource. She is at the furthest remove imaginable from the experimental writer; her technique is invisible; rather one has the sense of an organic form constantly renewing itself to meet the various challenges of experience. Her perpetual transfiguration of the ordinary make her pre-

eminently the heir to the Joyce of *Dubliners.*

The indisputable heir to Daniel Corkery in the short story is Bryan MacMahon (b.1909) whose wide-ranging talents have encompassed three Abbey plays, *The Bugle in the Blood* (1949), *The Song of the Anvil* (1960) and *The Honey Spike* (1961) — which appeared as a novel in 1967 — and a remarkable prose idyll, *Children of the Rainbow* (1952). His short stories, *The Lion Tamer* (1948) and *The Red Petticoat* (1955) are infused with a powerful sense of place and a poignant nostalgia for traditional life patterns under threat from materialism and mass culture. Francis MacManus (1909-65) also began his career with a fictional investigation of Corkery's 'Hidden Ireland' in his trilogy on the 18th-century Gaelic poet, Donnacha Ruadh MacConmara, before he turned to the sensitive realism of his contemporary novels, notably *Watergate* (1942) and his scene of clerical life *The Greatest of These* (1943). The Ulster writer, Michael McLaverty (b.1907), evinces a similar affection for the quiet moments in Irish rural existence, a lyrical sense of landscape in such short story collections as *The White Mare* (1943) and *The Game Cock* (1949) and novels like *Lost Fields* and *Call my Brother Back.*

The Thirties ended with the resounding fracture of inherited literary forms. The publication of Joyce's *Finnegans Wake* in 1939 marked the outer limits of experiment with language, while Beckett's *Murphy* (1938) and Flann O'Brien's *At Swim Two Birds* (1939) broke the moulds of form with two brilliantly dissimilar novels of absurdity, wherein the conventions of realism are invoked only to be mocked, the sequence of narrative made to enact its own parody, and the world within the mind set at odds with the world outside it. The Second World War obscured the radical achievement of both writers. But while the crucible of the Resistance refined Beckett's metaphysic so that he emerged in terms of absolute greatness, Ireland's isolation and the lack of a publisher deflected O'Brien's creative energies into journalism which, however brilliant, was an evasion of the real artistic challenge. His second and finest novel, *The Third Policeman,*

46
47

Some of the notable Irish women writers of this century:

48
49

The Contemporary Phase

46 *Elisabeth Bowen (1900-73)*
by G M B Holland.

47 *Mary Lavin (b. 1912).*

48 *Edna O'Brien (b. 1936).*

49 *Val Mulkerns (b. 1925).*

50 *Kate Cruise O'Brien (b. 1948)*

51 *Julia O'Faoláin (b. 1932).*

52 *Jennifer Johnson (b. 1930).*

53 *Eavan Boland (b. 1945).*

50
51

52
53

written in 1940 was not published till after his death in 1966 at the age of fifty four. Since then he has become a cult figure in the universities and among those novelists, British and American, who have developed an esthetic of parody and solipsism in the fictional form. Samuel Beckett (b.1906) moved into his great phase as a prose writer with *Watt* (1945) which was followed by his astonishing trilogy, *Molloy; Malone Dies; The Unnamable,* published in English translation by the author 1959.

Perhaps the most typical figure of the Forties was Mervyn Wall (b.1908) who confronted the bleakness and isolation of the decade in terms of radical satire with his *Unfortunate Fursey* (1946) and its hilarious sequel, *The Return of Fursey* (1948). Taking a hint perhaps from the prose romances of Austin Clarke, Wall situated his fictions in medieval Ireland 'where anything can happen to any one, at any time, in any place; and it usually does,' and chose for his hero a little monk of invincible innocence. Through this mythic world, Wall refracts his vision of Modern Ireland and its limitations, anatomising clericalism, censorship, obscurantism, hypocrisy, jansenism, complacency, nepotism. In *Leaves for the Burning* (1952), he engages these issues in terms of realism, where the squalid adventures of four educated Irishmen on a drunken spree are counterpointed against the return of Yeats' remains for interment at Drumcliff, romantic Ireland having been thoroughly killed and buried in the interim.

Another shrewd obituarist of the Gaelic dream was James Plunkett (b.1920) whose fine collection of short stories, *The Trusting and the Maimed* (1959) portrayed the Dublin of the late Forties in a manner reminiscent of Joyce's *Dubliners:* a vision at once sympathetic and mordant in which idealistic young clerks go to seed in gloomy offices and sordid pubs, in which the Irish language is beaten into hungry and deprived children and in which love seems doomed by the hopelessness of society. Plunkett's two panoramic historical novels, *Strumpet City* (1969) and its sequel, *Farewell, Companions* (1977), chronicle the development of Irish society from the beginning of the century through a perspective considerably more benign than that of the short

stories, though still striking for its fidelity to the social world it depicts.

In the Fifties, the critique of society continued to be a major pre-occupation of the novel. In works like *The Hard Man* (1958) and *The Devil You Know* (1962), WJ White mounted a witty commentary on the new managerial classes which were emerging as the age of De Valera yielded to the more pragmatic policies of Lemass. Terence de Vere White (b.1912) began his career with satiric autobiography, *The Fretful Midge* (1957) in which the course of Dublin social values over a couple of decades is cunningly exposed; and in his subsequent novels and short stories he remains sharply alert to the nuances of an increasingly metamorphic social scene. By contrast Val Mulkerns (b.1925) in her first novel, *A Time Outworn* (1950), has left a most memorable imaginative record of adolescence in the Dublin of her times. The Belfast writer, Janet MacNeill (b.1907) in novels like *A Child in the House* (1955) and *The Maiden Dinosaur* (1964) also concentrated most intensely on the private and the personal.

The major talents to emerge in the decade were, however, Benedict Kiely and Brian Moore. Kiely (b.1919) represents, in a way, the emergence of a new generation from the quarantine of the war years. The theme of his early novels, written in the late Forties and early Fifties, is rather like that of Clarke in his 'straying student' syndrome. In dramatising the struggle in the mind of his young heroes — often clerical students — between the flesh and the spirit, Kiely pointed the way for Edna O'Brien, McGahern and Broderick in the following decade. These stories of personal crisis, *Land without Stars* (1946) and *There Was an Ancient House* (1955) yielded to the even more successful *Cards of the Gambler* (1953) a brilliant experiment with the morphology of a folktale and his powerful study in selfishness, *The Captain with The Whiskers* (1960). His most recent fiction has been a dramatic novella, *Proxopera* (1978) provoked by the current horrors in his native Tyrone. This same theme of Northern violence is caught with comparable power by Eugene McCabe (b.1930) in his short novel *Victims* (1976); his remarkable play, *King of the*

Castle had been one of the great theatrical successes of the Sixties.

Brian Moore (b.1921) began his career with what is still regarded as one of his finest novels, *Judith Hearne* (1955), a study of religious guilt, alcoholism, loneliness and sexual frustration in a Belfast spinster's existence. Moore's gift with female psychology has reappeared in his brilliant *Answer from Limbo* (1960) and *I am Mary Dunne* (1968) both of which have North American settings. His *Bildungsroman, The Emperor of Ice-Cream* (1965), investigates the growth of self-awareness in the mind of a young Belfastman during the Second World War, his painful withdrawal from his religious and nationalistic loyalties, his estrangement from and reconcilement with his father a relation that haunts the Moore hero whether he is in Belfast or California.

The Sixties were remarkable not only for the number of arresting new talents, McGahern, Casey, Edna O'Brien, Higgins, Power, Leitch, West, Broderick, Trevor, but for the late flowering of several senior novelists, Michael Farrell, Monk Gibbon, Patrick Boyle, above all Francis Stuart. Farrell's one massive novel, *Thy Tears Might Cease* after a lifetime's gestation, was triumphantly edited by his friend Monk Gibbon and published to acclaim in 1963. It is equalled in its generation only by Plunkett's in sweep and range. Monk Gibbon (b.1896) who had been writing distinguished poetry, autobiography and criticism for half a century had a marvellous creative upsurge, producing his sensitive novel, *The Climate of Love* (1961), and his superb memoir of the Great War, *Inglorious Soldier* (1968), before the decade was out. Patrick Boyle (b.1905) was even more remarkable. Having taken up fiction as a young man he had abandoned it for a career in the bank until in his mid fifties he produced his tragi-comic masterpiece, *Like Any Other Man,* (1966) in which he skillfully invoked the Samson myth to underpin the tragedy of a drunken, lecherous bank manager trapped and destroyed by a love passion in a small provincial town. Since its great success, Boyle has devoted himself to the short story in such volumes as *At Night all Cats are*

Grey (1966) and *All Looks Yellow to the Jaundiced Eye* (1969), the former containing a story of lost innocence entitled 'The Betrayers' which ranks with the finest in that form.

The decade was, notwithstanding, dominated by such adventurous younger talents as Edna O'Brien, John McGahern, Aidan Higgins, Richard Power, Kevin Casey and John Broderick. Edna O'Brien (b. 1936) disconcerted the Irish reading public, and intrigued the world outside, with the sexual candour of her two poignant first novels, *The Country Girls* (1960) and *The Lonely Girls* (1962). The phenomenon of a well-bred convent girl from Clare discoursing with such frankness on country matters at a time when such topics were largely left to the men — even in the world outside — not only drew the vengeance of the Censor, but blinded sensible critics and readers to the books' literary merits, their delicate psychological insight, the fluent simplicity of the prose and effortless mastery of narrative. The three books that immediately followed are usually deemed inferior, dealing as they do with recent, less digested, cosmopolitan experience. But her short stories, *The Love Object* (1970) and *A Scandalous Woman* (1974) contrive to capture those isolated moments of intense experience which these middle novels fail to fix in permanent form. Even in the shorter form, however, it is in those mysterious bonds with her home and family that her best opportunities occur, as in that small masterpiece 'Cords'. Her most recent novels, notably *A Pagan Place* (1970) and *Night* (1972) return to the scenes of her early work for theme and inspiration.

John McGahern (b.1935) also fell foul of the Censor in his second book, *The Dark* (1965). Arguably the controversy over his and Edna O'Brien's work broke the already slackening grip of the censorship over Irish literature. McGahern had begun his career with a powerful first novel, *The Barracks* (1963), a study of conflict and frustration set in the confined arena of a police station in rural Ireland. The bleak honesty with which he exposes the operation of human love, erotic and familial, in *The Barracks* is carried into his subsequent fictions: *The Dark* examines the perverse domination of a son by a father and its psychic consequences for both; *The Leavetaking* (1974) is part a study of sexual love, part an obsessive return to the hero's shaping experiences in the landscape of the first novel. The short story collections, *Night Lines* (1973) and *Getting Through* (1978) divide the emphasis of their fiction between these two imaginative worlds producing works of equivalent power from each: the macabre childhood epiphanies of 'Night Lines' and 'The Bomb Box' sounding within the same consciousness in antiphon with 'My Love, My Umbrella' and 'Along the Edges'.

Kevin Casey's first novel — it remains the best of the three he has published — *The Sinner's Bell* equals anything in McGahern for mordancy of vision. Its opening scene, the wedding of a young middle-class couple in a provincial town, and the squalid honeymoon in London that follows, foreshadow a married life in which the sensitive bride is trapped, ignored and humiliated by the casual barbarism of economics, religion, society, and local attitudes to marriage itself.
Without recourse to overt satire, *The Sinner's Bell* is probably the most desolating image of married life, and of a certain Irish male temperament, in contemporary fiction.

Aidan Higgins (b.1927) seems to write out of a conscious sense of despair which gives unforgettable poignancy to his account of human relationships. His first two works were *Felo de Se* (1960), a collection of short stories, and *Langrishe Go Down,* his splendid novel of defeated love and dynastic decay set in a run-down Catholic mansion in Kildare. Its sense of atmosphere, its account of the love affair between the cold German student and the aging spinster and the strange eloquence of its language make it one of the most memorable of modern novels. John Broderick, also born in 1927, has concentrated his vision on the works and days of the Irish midlands where he has found the shopkeepers, priests, professional men and entrepeneurs who make up the dubious *dramatis personae* of his fiction — proof positive that 'silence, exile and cunning' are no longer a necessity even for the satirist. This provincial world could now almost be called 'Broderick country' by virtue of the six substantial novels he has quarried from its social landscape. In *The Pilgrimage* (1961), *The Fugitives* (1962), *The Waking of Willie Ryan* (1965) and most provokingly in *The Pride of Summer* (1976) he has evolved a form of fiction peculiar to himself, a blend of realism, moralism and satire in which the author goes to war with his milieu and himself. When the blend works the result is a fine dark comedy; mischief and sympathy held weirdly in suspension; and it often works. Richard Power (1928-70) had a tragically short writing career. His first novel, *The Land of Youth,* an original but uneven work set in the early decades of the century appeared when he was thirty-six. His second and last, *The Hungry Grass* (1969), published in the year before his death, comes very close to perfection, in structure, mood, atmosphere and characterisation; its central figure, Father Conroy, is probably the most rounded and credible portrait of a priest in Irish fiction. William Trevor (b.1928) was also a late furnisher, but once started he has shown notable stamina and inventiveness. Like Elizabeth Bowen, whose Anglo-Irish background he shares, Trevor has shaped his best novels out of English experience and his best short stories from Irish recollections. *Mrs Eckdorf in O'Neill's Hotel* is a shallow book by comparison with his first two English novels, *The Old Boys* and *The Boarding House* while the short stories of Irish life — 'The Distant Past', 'The Ballroom of Romance', 'An Evening with John Joe Dempsey' — are among his most accomplished work.

John Jordan (b.1930) has written one good but uneven collection of stories, *Yarns* (1977), and two volumes of lyric poetry, *Patrician Stations* (1971) and *A Raft for Flotsam* (1975), while a revival of publishing in Dublin has brought forward such recent talents as Neil Jordan, Kate Cruise O'Brien, Ronan Sheehan, Desmond Hogan and Maura Treacy.

It may seem odd to enter Francis Stuart (b.1902) at this late stage of the survey when the Sixties are yielding to the present decade; but there are good reasons. His maverick career makes best sense when viewed in retrospect, and furthermore he was

The Contemporary Phase

accepted for the first time into the centre of the mainstream of Irish letters with the publication of his challenging autobiographical novel, *Black List, Section H* (1971). This remarkable book embodied and dramatised his doctrine that the artist must live dangerously on the frontiers of orthodox experience. It revealed a unique personality, gambler, mystic, artist, revolutionary and a personal history involving marriage to Iseult Gonne (he is the 'dunce' libelled by Yeats in 'Why Should not Old Men be Mad'), internment by the Free State and 'defection' to Nazi Germany at the outbreak of World War II. The book was swiftly followed by a brilliant new novel, *Memorial* (1973) probing the same obsessive themes of love, sanctity and risk, against the background of the Northern troubles. From this vantage point it is possible to appreciate that impressive succession of novels, nineteen in all, in Stuart's canon, beginning with *Women and God* (1931) and including such outstanding fiction as *The Pillar of Cloud* (1948) set among the ruins of Europe, and *Redemption* (1974) which explores themes of faith, love, murder and forgiveness in a provincial Irish town.

The most assured novelists to emerge in the present decade have been John Banville, Julia O'Faolain and Jennifer Johnston. Banville (b.1946) revealed in his first book of related stories, *Long Lankin* (1970), a strikingly experimental approach to form, a mode of apprehension in which the active creative faculty became the most visible agent in the fiction. The same reflexive method governs his next two novels, *Nightspawn* (1971) and *Birchwood* (1973) where the real landscape of Wexford appears in startling counterpoint to the surreal landscape of the author's mind. But his finest book is surely his fourth, *Doctor Copernicus* (1972), where the life of the great astronomer gives him a theme ideally responsive to his curious genius.

Julia O'Faoláin (b.1932) also began with short stories and proceeded through one realistic novel — *Codded and Godded* (1970) — to her fine historical fiction, *Women in the Wall* (1975). Her two short story collections, *We Might See Sights* (1978) and *Man in the Cellar* (1974) with their

epiphanies of an Irish childhood — she lives in California — vindicate her father's doctrine that Mnemosyne is the particular muse of the short story.

Jennifer Johnston — also born to the purple of Irish letters —,made a spectacular impact on the critics and the marketplace with her first three short novels, *The Captains and the Kings,* (1972), *The Gates* (1973) and her novel of the First World War, *How Many Miles to Babylon?* (1974). Whatever her overt theme, love between an old man and a boy or the horrors of the trenches, Jennifer Johnston seems to have one central concern over which the imagination lyrically broods — the decay of the great houses of Ireland and the values they embodied. The line runs down to her from Maria Edgeworth.

54

Conclusion

To glance back to the beginnings of our summary and to trace its curve over three hundred years is to note above all how intimately literature consorts with historical process, both as cause and effect. Each of the four phases sketched here takes its character from historical developments and events — The Sixth of George the First, the Act of Union, The Rise of Young Ireland, the founding of the new state. One could argue that each of these events involved a shift in human sensibility which then found expression in new literary impulses and constructs. It could be argued as persuasively that the literature first changed men's minds and that those men by their actions changed the course of history. Yeats asked memorably:

Did that play of mine send out
Certain men the English shot?

But we might ask with equal validity whether that play of his would have been written in the first place had not certain men the English jailed, like John O'Leary, come to influence the young poet in his most formative years.

The second observation one might make is how the fortunes of the two languages are related to the development of their respective literatures. The success story of Anglo-Irish literature as defined here almost constitutes the reflex action of the native Irish literature in its decline and fall. Carleton's progress from the obscurity of his bilingual peasant culture of Co. Tyrone to the celebrity of a literary career in Dublin involved a turning away from the ancestral language. The choice takes many similar forms in the century that follows. In our own time we can instance Liam O'Flaherty, born into an Irish speaking community on Inis Mór, whose one Irish collection of stories, *Dúil,* stands in plaintive contrast to his immense output in the English language. The loss of the Irish language has been grievous, and its implications for the Irish writer, incalcuable. The boast that England gave us a language and we gave them back a literature is only a partial consolation. Yet it would be hard to condemn outright a development that has given us the drama of Synge and O'Casey, the poetry of Kavanagh and Heaney and the prose of James Joyce; especially as Joyce has taken such a savage vengeance on the language of the stranger in his Schonbergian swansong, *Finnegans Wake.*

A third dimension of irony is, of course, added by the fact that while Irish-speaking Ireland struggled into the light — or the dark, as some would have it — of literacy in the English language, English-speaking, Ascendency Ireland was struggling backwards towards Gaelic roots and origins. A line of scholars from Charlotte Brooke through Standish Hayes O'Grady to Osborn Bergin laboured to disinter ballad and story, rann and song, epic, lyric and legend from the buried heritage of old Ireland while a line of poets from Ferguson, through Sigerson, Yeats and Lady Gregory down to Clarke and Kinsella in present times presented Cuchulain, Maeve, Fergus, Fionn, Niamh and Oisín to a world which would not otherwise know of their existence.

It was no wonder therefore that the young Pearse should have so bitterly attacked the Irish Literary Theatre on its first appearance at the the turn of the present century. He feared that Anglo-Irish literature might cut the ground from under the Irish language movement by appropriating its most cherished mythologies and presenting them to the world in English. But Pearse was soon reconciled and came to see the Literary Revival as a means of bridging the gap between the two Irish nations.

Our story began with those two nations sharply distinct one Irish-speaking, traditional Catholic and enslaved; the other English-speaking, modern, Protestant and Ascendent; two literatures, that of Swift, that of Dáibhí Ó Bruadair; the one modern, enlightened, rational, energetic, the other bitterly articulate with the elegies of a defeated culture; each operating on a small island in almost total ignorance of the other. Today that small island is divided by a political boundary but the literary culture is now held in common: the republic of Irish letters is one. John Hewitt and John Montague share the same tradition, and share it to a considerable degree with their fellow poets in the Irish language, Martin Ó Direáin, Máire Mac an tSaoi, Seán

Anglo-Irish Literature

Ó Riordáin, Eoin Ó Tuairisc. A short poem by John $\quad$ 54
Hewitt, Protestant, planter and patriot, who came
from the peace of the English midlands to live out his
retirement at home in strife-ridden Belfast makes a
fitting coda to a complicated history:

There's not a chance now that I might recover
one syllable of what that sick man said,
tapping upon my great-grandmother's shutter,
and begging, I was told, a piece of bread;
for on his tainted breath there hung infection
rank from the cabins of the stricken west,
the spores from black potato-stalks, the spittle
mottled with poison in his rattling chest;
but she who, by her nature, quickly answered,
accepted in return the famine-fever;
and that chance meeting, that brief confrontation,
conscribed me of the Irishry forever.

Though much I cherish lies outside their vision,
and much they prize I have no claim to share,
yet in that woman's death I found my nation;
the old wound aches and shews its fellow-scar.

('The Scar' from *Out of my Time* by John Hewitt,
Blackstaff Press, Belfast, 1974).

54 *Dancer by Louis Le Broquy*
from The Tain, *series.*

Select Bibliography

Boyd, Ernest A, *Ireland's Literary Renaissance* (London 1922)
Boyd, Ernest A, *The contemporary Drama in Ireland,* (Boston 1917)
Brown, Malcolm, *The Politics of Irish Literature* (London 1972)
Brown, Terence, *Northern Voices,* (Dublin 1975)
Clarke, Austin, *Poetry in Modern Ireland* (Dublin 1951)
Corkery, Daniel, *The Hidden Ireland* (Dublin 1956)
Cronin, John, *The Anglo-Irish Novel,* Vol. 1, The Nineteenth Century (Belfast 1980)
Flanagan, Thomas, *The Irish Novelists 1800-1850* (New York, 1959)
Harmon, Maurice, *Select Bibliography for the Study of Anglo-Irish Literature and Backgrounds:*
              an Irish Studies Handbook, Dublin 1977
Hoagaland, Kathleen, *1000 Years of Irish Poetry,* (New York 1947)
Hogan, Robert, ed., *Dictionary of Irish Literature* (Dublin 1980)
Hunt, Hugh, *The Abbey, Ireland's National Theatre, 1904-1979* (Dublin 1975)
Howarth, Herbert, *The Irish Writers 1800-1940* (New York 1959)
Kennelly, Brendan, *The Penguin Book of Irish Verse,* (London 1970)
Kiely, Benedict, *Modern Irish Fiction, a Critique* (Dublin 1950)
Mercier, Vivian and Greene, David, eds. *1000 Years of Irish Prose* (New York 1947)
Montague, John, *The Faber Book of Irish Verse* (London 1974)
Moore, George, *Hail and Farewell* (London 1911)
Rafroidi, Patrick and Brown, Terence, eds., *The Irish Short Story* (Gerrards Cross 1980)
Rafroidi, Patrick and Harmon, Maurice, eds., *The Irish Novel in Our Time* (Lille 1976)
Welch, Robert, *Irish Poetry from Moore to Yeats* (Gerrards Cross 1980)
Yeats, W B *Autobiographies* (London 1914)

Index

Anglo-Irish Literature

Photographic Credits

The Department of Foreign Affairs would like to thank the
following for their assistance with illustrations used
in the book:

Courtesy of the Abbey Theatre	26, 17
Robert Ballagh	1, 4, 20, 22, 23, 30, 37, 39, 40, 42, 44
Courtesy of the Chester Beatty Library	16
Mike Bunn	33, 34
Seamus Cashman, Wolfhound Press	41
Courtesy of Mr Finlay Colley	46
Deegan Photo	26, 27, 46
Mark Gerson	51
Courtesy of Hardwicke, Dublin	Cover
J & S Harsch	36, 43
The Irish Times	31, 48
Desmond Kinney	Cover
Courtesy of Eleanor Kinsella	35
Mary Lavin	47
Courtesy of Philip MacDermott Ltd.	44
Martin Nangle	52
National Gallery of Ireland	5, 7, 9, 13, 17, 18, 19, 28
National Library of Ireland	10, 14, 25, 29
Courtesy of the National Portrait Gallery, London	236
Courtesy of The O'Brien Press	33, 34
Courtesy of the Oriel Gallery	24
Pan Books	45 d, f
Penguin Books	45 c, e, g, h, j
Pieterse Davison International Ltd.	16
Poolbeg Press	45, 49, 50 b, i, l
Poolbeg/Quartet	45 a, k
Breffni Ryan	53
Patrick Scott	54
John Taylor Gallery	55